SO-AFV-223

BFI FILM CLASSICS

. . . .

Rob White
SERIES EDITOR

Colin MacCabe and David Meeker
SERIES CONSULTANTS

Cinema is a fragile medium. Many of the great classic films of the past now exist, if at all, in damaged or incomplete prints. Concerned about the deterioration in the physical state of our film heritage, the National Film and Television Archive, a Division of the British Film Institute, has compiled a list of 360 key films in the history of the cinema. The long-term goal of the Archive is to build a collection of perfect showprints of these films, which will then be screened regularly at the Museum of the Moving Image in London in a year-round repertory.

BFI Film Classics is a series of books commissioned to stand alongside these titles. Authors, including film critics and scholars, film-makers, novelists, historians and those distinguished in the arts, have been invited to write on a film of their choice, drawn from the Archive's list. Each volume presents the author's own insights into the chosen film, together with a brief production history and a detailed filmography, notes and bibliography. The numerous illustrations have been specially made from the Archive's own prints.

With new titles published each year, the BFI Film Classics series will rapidly grow into an authoritative and highly readable guide to the great films of world cinema.

Could scarcely be improved upon ... informative, intelligent, jargon-free companions.
The Observer

Cannily but elegantly packaged BFI Classics will make for a neat addition to the most discerning shelves.
New Statesman & Society

WEST BEND LIBRARY

BFI FILM CLASSICS

HIGH NOON

. . . .

Phillip Drummond

BRITISH FILM INSTITUTE

bfi

BFI PUBLISHING

First published in 1997 by the
BRITISH FILM INSTITUTE
21 Stephen Street, London W1P 2LN

Copyright © Phillip Drummond 1997

The British Film Institute exists
to promote appreciation, enjoyment, protection and
development of moving image culture in and throughout the
whole of the United Kingdom.
Its activities include the National Film and
Television Archive; the National Film Theatre;
the Museum of the Moving Image;
the London Film Festival; the production and
distribution of film and video; funding and support for
regional activities; Library and Information Services;
Stills, Posters and Designs; Research;
Publishing and Education; and the monthly
Sight and Sound magazine.

British Library Cataloguing-in-Publication Data
A catalogue record for this book is available from the British Library

ISBN 0–85170–494–8

Designed by
Andrew Barron & Collis Clements Associates

Typesetting by
D R Bungay Associates, Burghfield, Berks.

Printed in Great Britain by Norwich Colour Printers

791.4372
H536d

CONTENTS

. . . .

*In loving memory of my mother Linda Drummond
(née Rowlands), 1920 -1995*

ACKNOWLEDGMENTS
. . . .

My warmest gratitude goes to Fred Zinnemann for his willingness to watch *High Noon* with me, and for giving so freely of his time and self for a discussion of his work in Hollywood during the post-war period. His personal generosity taught me a great deal, and made my research a huge pleasure, if a yet more awesome obligation.

I am also grateful to those officers of the BFI who ensured that this volume saw the light of day: to Ed Buscombe, a great editor, for commissioning this book and for his patience in nursing it to a conclusion; to David Meeker, for his practical support throughout the project; and to Rob White, for taking over the final editorial burden with sympathy and care.

INTRODUCTION

. . . .

High Noon tells, it seems, a simple tale. It is a hot Sunday morning sometime late in the 19th century. Will Kane, the retiring marshal of the small town of Hadleyville, somewhere in western America, is marrying his Quaker bride, Amy, and leaving with her for a new life in another place. News arrives that Frank Miller, a notorious outlaw whom Kane had put away for life, has been paroled after only five years in jail and is arriving on the noon train to fulfil his threat to seek revenge, abetted by three sidekicks who have already arrived in town. The marshal is initially persuaded to leave as planned, but it is not long before he feels obliged to turn back, even though his new bride cannot understand, or support, his instinctive need to confront Miller. She abandons him in order to catch the noon train back home to St Louis.

For the next hour or so of screen time, the marshal attempts to recruit new deputies, but a fearful, sometimes hypocritical and even partly jubilant town leaves him to face his fate alone. After writing his will, and filled with fear, he takes on the gang in a deadly game of hide-and-seek in the empty streets of Hadleyville. Hearing the first gunshot as she boards the train, Amy undergoes a change of heart and returns; putting aside her religious principles, she shoots an outlaw in the back and kills him. Further helped by Amy, who has been taken hostage, Kane goes on to win the final showdown with Miller. Throwing down his star, he leaves the town a second time with Amy as the townsfolk gather in embarrassment and wonder.

This apparently straightforward story is, however, not just words on the page but a complex, tense and urgent flow of moving images and sounds. It centres on a major cultural icon of the period, Gary Cooper, here summarising and revising his long history of cinematic stardom since the 1920s, and generating complex images of troubled masculinity along the way. As an audio-visual tale, it is also a conspicuously generic construct. It is a 'western', with all the mythic meanings of tales set in the history of the North American West, told for the pleasure of the mid-twentieth-century cinema audience. It is an American film, made within the realms of Hollywood cinema, and yet Hollywood cinema of a particular kind – the independent cinema of the post-war years, of Fred Zinnemann, Stanley Kramer, and Carl Foreman.

As a particular kind of Hollywood text, it is marked by its relationship to the changing cinematic conditions of the early 1950s, and by the Cold War politics which find a variety of parallels in the film's plot and led directly to the sacrifice of its screenwriter amid the frenzied witch-hunts of the House Committee on Un-American Activities (HUAC). Above all, it is a film about ethics and morality, and their intersection with the social world of citizens and law and order – themes which, endearing *High Noon* to successive generations of the world audience, including US Presidents from Eisenhower to Clinton, draw the film out of the fifties and project a longer and more complex vision of the cultural and ideological role of popular cinema.

1

AUTHORS

Fred Zinnemann

Fred Zinnemann, the director of *High Noon*, was born in Vienna in 1907, where he studied law at the university. Abandoning the prospect of a legal career, he trained at the Technical School of Cinema in Paris and became a cameraman in Paris and Berlin, working on a number of films, including Robert Siodmak's *People on Sunday* (1929). He emigrated to the US in October 1929, arriving on the day of the Wall Street crash. He found work as an extra on Milestone's *All Quiet on the Western Front* (1930), as a cutter, and as an assistant to Robert Flaherty (on an uncompleted project), Berthold Viertel (on *The Man from Yesterday*, 1932) and Busby Berkeley (*The Kid from Spain*, 1932). He made his debut as director on *The Wave* (1934), produced by Paul Strand, a Flaherty-influenced documentary about the lives of fishermen on the Gulf Coast of Mexico. In 1937 he was signed by MGM as a director of shorts, where he contributed eighteen items to such series as *Crime Does Not Pay* and *Historical Mysteries*, many characterised by innovatory optical effects. In 1938 he won the studio an Oscar for *That Mothers Might Live*.[1]

He became a feature director in the 1940s, turning out a number of B-pictures under a seven-year contract with MGM. These included *Kid Glove Killer* (1942) with Van Heflin, Marsha Hunt and Lee Bowman, a police procedural in which crime-lab workers pit their forensic skills against the forces of political corruption; *Eyes in the Night* (1942), about a blind detective who uncovers and destroys a Nazi spy-ring; and two 1947 vehicles for the child-star 'Butch' Jenkins, *Little Mister Jim* and *My Brother Talks to Horses*. Zinnemann's next four films dealt with the run-up to and aftermath of war. His first A-picture was *The Seventh Cross* (1944), a film starring Spencer Tracy set in prewar Nazi Germany about a group of prisoners on the run from a concentration camp, all failing to escape but one. Zinnemann remembered this as a fore-shadowing of *High Noon*: 'in a country gone berserk a man is running for his life, unable to

trust anyone except former friends who are endangered by *his mere presence*'.[2] In the course of WWII Zinnemann was loaned by MGM to the Swiss producer Lazar Wechsler to make *The Search* (1948), filmed in Germany and Switzerland, centring on a war orphan's quest to find his mother and to regain the power of speech. Introducing Montgomery Clift, *The Search* won Oscars for its screenplay and for its child star, Ivan Jandl. *Act of Violence* (1948) was Zinnemann's last contract picture for MGM, a post-war *film noir* in which a former POW (Robert Ryan) hunts down a former fellow inmate (Van Heflin) who has sacrificed his comrades to save his own skin. *The Men* (1950), Zinnemann's intimate account for Stanley Kramer and United Artists of the tribulations of wounded veterans, introduced Marlon Brando, fresh from the Broadway success of *A Streetcar Named Desire*, as the paraplegic soldier who must face the task of rebuilding his marriage and his life. It was followed by *Teresa* (1951), made for Arthur Loew at MGM. *Teresa* is a film about the 'war bride' issue of the post-war period in which a young American

The Search: Zinnemann with
Montgomery Clift and Ivan Jandl

Masculinity impaired and under scrutiny: Marlon Brando and Everett Sloane in *The Men*

1 2   The intercultural couple: John Ericsson and Pier Angeli in *Teresa*

soldier brings home an Italian wife. It stars Pier Angeli and John
Ericsson, and introduces Rod Steiger. As in *The Search*, the film's
troubled European locations – in this case Livergnano, Siena and the
mountains between Florence and Bologna – are highly expressive. As
with *The Men*, 'There was to be an open ending ... the traditional wish-
dream of marriage as a guarantee of permanent happiness would be put
in question'.[3]

High Noon, with its own discourse on marriage between a man and
a woman from different cultures, was made in 1951, released in 1952 and
in 1953 earned four Oscars and made Zinnemann the New York Critics'
director of the year. In 1953, Zinnemann completed his three-picture
deal with Kramer by directing *The Member of the Wedding*, based on
Carson McCullers' Deep South novel and subsequent Broadway hit
about a lonely young girl (Julie Harris) and her subjective involvement
in her brother's wedding. In the same year, *From Here to Eternity*, his
critical drama about life in the US military during the period of Pearl
Harbour, projected Frank Sinatra to stardom and garnered a total of
eight Oscars. This major box office success catapulted Zinnemann into
the front rank of major American directors.

Adult rituals, childhood fantasies: Julie Harris and Ethel Waters in *Member of the Wedding*   1 3

Zinnemann thus brought distinctive authorial experience and preoccupations to *High Noon*. His long training in the studio-bound industry of the 1930s and 1940s, particularly his work on the MGM shorts, gave him a conscious commitment to density and economy. At the same time, he was drawn to the freedom of post-war independent cinema, and to the very different kind of production platform provided by Kramer: low-budget, intensive, small-scale. Independent production also provided him with the opportunity for a new kind of social and aesthetic realism; with his intimate use of location and non-professional actors his work comes close at moments to the concerns of contemporary European neo-realism. A dramatist of moral crisis, his varied subject-matter – from *High Noon* to *A Nun's Story* (1959) and onwards to *A Man for All Seasons* (1966) – cohered around what Richard Schickel was to call 'unblinking studies in threatened integrity'.[4]

1 4   The spectacle of film production: Zinnemann shooting *From Here to Eternity*

Stanley Kramer

Born in New York in 1913, Kramer had worked in films since the mid-1930s as a researcher, film editor and writer. Following war service with the US Army Signal Corps, he began his cycle of low-budget but prestigious 'message' pictures. He was to become the key innovatory new producer in the post-war drive for independence as the studio system underwent massive change and upheaval. A total of seventeen films were to follow between 1948 and 1954 as Kramer created his own mini-studio at the Motion Picture Center, based on a small team of regular contributors. Ralph Sternad served as production designer on all seventeen films; Dimitri Tiomkin scored almost half; Franz Planer shot nearly a third. Thirteen of the films were directed by just five directors – Edward Dmytryk (four), Fred Zinnemann (three), Laszlo Benedek, Richard Fleischer and Mark Robson (two each). Scripts for six were created by Carl Foreman prior to his rift with Kramer during *High Noon* in Autumn 1951.[5]

A low-budget ethos, combined with liberal social values, were to be the hallmarks of Kramer's approach. A commitment to experiment was balanced by a frank reliance on the tried and tested stage-play; nearly half the seventeen films came straight from the theatre, a strategic choice which Kramer openly attributed to a distrust of writers and a preference for the security of the dramatic text. Intensive methods for production involved preparation for as long as a year per picture, culminating in short bursts of intensive rehearsal with players and technicians. Shooting schedules were usually as short as three to six weeks. *High Noon* rehearsed for a week and was shot in a month, whilst *Home*

of the Brave, bought in mid-January 1949, was shot in a mere eighteen days, and the first print was ready at the beginning of April for release in late May, creating something of a record for the independent cinema. Profits could be substantial for Kramer's backers: in 1950 Robert Stillman was happy to report a profit of $500,000 on his investment of $347,000 in *Champion* and *Home of the Brave*.[6]

Kramer's first film, Fleischer's *So This Is New York* (1948), starred Henry Morgan in a social comedy about inherited wealth, marriage, and the differing life styles of Indiana and New York. It was followed by Robson's *Champion*, a *film noir* about boxing, which starred Kirk Douglas and, nominated for five Academy Awards, won an Oscar for its editor Harry Gerstad. Robson's *Home of the Brave*, made in secrecy in two months in the Spring of 1949, turned Arthur Laurents' play about anti-Semitism in the US Army into a groundbreaking account of army racism, focusing on the psychological history of a wounded black GI, played by James Edwards. The theme of the traumatised male was further explored in Zinnemann's *The Men* (1950), and in Gordon's *Cyrano de Bergerac*, starring José Ferrer and released some six weeks before the start of *High Noon*. Masculinity in crisis was the persistent theme of Kramer's early career.

Kramer now moved from the margin to the centre by taking on a multi-picture deal with Columbia that would commit him to the hectic schedule of producing thirty films within five years, heralding a major change from the serial production practices of his earlier period. The first film in the deal, Benedek's screen version of Arthur Miller's *Death of a Salesman*, starring Frederic March, was released in Spring 1952, quickly followed by Fregonese's prison film *My Six Convicts*. *High Noon* was previewed at the end of April 1952, followed in May by *The Sniper*, a crime drama about a serial murderer (Arthur Franz), directed by Edward Dmytryk, just back from a HUAC jail sentence. Fleischer's *The Happy Time*, a comedy of manners chronicling the coming of age of a teenage boy (Bobby Driscoll) in the 1920s, Reis' *The Four Poster*, a two-hander based on Jan de Hartog's play about the progress of a married couple (Rex Harrison and Lilli Palmer) between the 1890s and the roaring twenties, and Dmytryk's *Eight Iron Men*, a war film about a group of soldiers who risk their lives to rescue a trapped comrade, were released in quick succession between December 1952 and January 1953.

Zinnemann's *The Member of the Wedding* was followed by Dmytryk's *The Juggler*, the story of the emotional and psychological recuperation of an entertainer (Kirk Douglas) who, after losing his wife and child in the concentration camps of the 1930s, goes to Israel as a post-war refugee. Rowland's *The 5,000 Fingers of Doctor T*, a technicolour musical fantasy in which a young boy (Tommy Rettig) falls asleep over his piano practice and dreams his way into a hellish underworld presided over by the fiendish Dr. Terwilliker (Hans Conreid), also appeared in 1953. Benedek's *The Wild One* (1954), one of several fifties pictures about youth in rebellion, and the generation gap, reintroduces Marlon Brando, this time as the leader of a motorcycle gang that disturbs the peace of a middle American town. Kramer's final film purely as producer was Dmytryk's *The Caine Mutiny* (1954), starring Humphrey Bogart as Captain Queeg in a story of power and delusion leading to a wartime mutiny aboard the USS Caine. Although the deal with Columbia was dissolved, Kramer went on to become one of the major producer/director figures of the later 1950s.

Kramer's early films are dour, bleak and sometimes grim dramas which do not shirk from addressing controversial issues – race, boxing as a commercial sport, the plight of war veterans, the treatment of criminals, youth culture and the power games of military life. The dramas occasionally focus on the world of the male or female child or adolescent, but they more usually deal with questions of identity and interpersonal relationship within the world of adults. In some, marriage is an important theme, but more usually an incomplete heterosexual romance is the fundamental dynamic (including the unconsummated marriage of *High Noon*). Masculine identity, and relations amongst men, are more central themes, and the male group with its powerful but troubled rituals is the commonest dramatic focus. Most frequently, the drama centres on the disturbed male individual caught up in wider systems of physical violence. Men who are incapacitated or even physically deformed will be key figures, as will those suffering psychological disturbances, who may need other male agents to control and treat them (policemen and psychiatrists are important subsidiary figures in these films). *High Noon*, the story of a honeymoon violently interrupted by male avengers from the past, is an archetypal Kramer film when seen within this context.

Carl Foreman

Carl Foreman, the writer of *High Noon* and also its original associate producer, was born in Chicago in 1914, the son of immigrants from Russia. He began as a circus and carnival promoter before becoming a freelance journalist, publicist, and eventually a gag writer for Eddie Cantor's radio shows. Nurtured by Dore Schary, he made his debut as a screenwriter in the early 1940s. He wrote three films for Monogram before joining Kramer – Fox's *Bowery Blitzkrieg* (1941), Rosen's *Spooks Run Wild* (1941) and Gould's *Rhythm Parade* (1942) – and provided the story for Kane's John Wayne vehicle, *Dakota* (1945), his only foray into the western genre prior to *High Noon*. After war duty with the US Army Signal Corps, he joined Kramer's company, writing screenplays for the producer's early excursions into serious, socially conscious film-making.[7]

Foreman wrote five films for Stanley Kramer between 1948 and 1951, becoming a partner in the company and acting as its treasurer. For Jerry Wald at Warner Brothers he also turned Dorothy Baker's novel about jazz musician Bix Beiderbecke into the screenplay for Curtiz's *Young Man with a Horn* (1950), co-written with Edmund H. North, and starring Douglas and Bacall. His other films of 1950 were *The Men* and *Cyrano de Bergerac*. Following the socio-historical comedy of *So This Is New York*, co-written with Herbert Baker from the novel by Ring Lardner, Foreman's screenplays for Kramer were dramas of gender and racial identity, notably *Champion* and *Home of the Brave*. Foreman's authorial role varied considerably across this body of work. It ranged from the original screenplay for *The Men* to screenplays based on such varying materials as 'stories' (*Champion*, *High Noon*), plays (*Cyrano*, *Home of the Brave*) and novels (*So This Is New York*, *Young Man with a Horn*). Between 1949 and 1952 his work was recognised by three Academy Award nominations – for *Champion*, *The Men*, and *High Noon*.

A number of Foreman themes provide a context for *High Noon*, his eleventh screenplay in just over a decade. Foreman had already worked on a not dissimilar concern in a seemingly very different film, *Cyrano de Bergerac*. In adapting Rostand's historic play about a misfit writer and his relationship with the community, Foreman can be seen to be commenting on the role of the writer in contemporary Hollywood. His additions to the play point up the power relations involved in the employment of a writer to create imaginary views of the world. *Cyrano* and *High Noon* can thus be seen as similar in the sense that in both films a distant period and a remote set of fictional conventions are deployed to dramatise contemporary social issues. More generally, the films are studies of men marked by identities which isolate them and cause them to re-examine and to re-interpret their understanding of their masculinity. Violent forms of contestation – notably war and boxing – are the arenas for this re-examination of virility and heroism. The body as a site for impairment and disfigurement looms large in *The Men* and in *Cyrano* as we prepare to meet the ageing and exhausted marshall of *High Noon*, played by the ailing Gary Cooper.[8]

Just as he was nearing a peak of personal prestige with the completion of his script for *High Noon*, however, Foreman's career was savagely interrupted by the latest anti-communist incursion into Hollywood by HUAC. In the middle of production on *High Noon* in September 1951, he appeared before the Committee as an 'unfriendly' witness and refused to confirm or deny membership of the Communist Party, to which he had in fact belonged from 1938 to 1942. Kramer promptly broke with him, and Foreman was obliged to relinquish his Associate Producer credit on *High Noon*. In early 1953 he effectively went into exile in England, where he resurfaced to write and produce powerful and thoughtful blockbusters (and became a Governor of the British Film Institute) before returning to the United States in 1975 to form a new independent company, named, with determined poignancy, 'High Noon'.

Floyd Crosby and Dimitri Tiomkin

Decisive in the development of an innovatory visual style for the film was director of cinematography Floyd Crosby, who had worked on documentaries with Flaherty, Lorentz and Ivens in the 1930s and had won an Oscar for the Murnau/Flaherty *Tabu* in 1931. A close friend of Zinnemann's since the latter's early days in the US, he had turned to Hollywood features in the 1950s, starting with Rossen's *The Brave Bulls* (1951). The intricate flow of Crosby's images is indebted to the skill of editors Harry Gerstad and Elmo Williams, while Kramer's resident production designer Ralph Sternad was an experienced contributor to the production of the film's historical 'look'. The wistful dynamic of the film's music track, and its poignant hit title song, were provided by Kramer's resident composer Dimitri Tiomkin. Born in the Ukraine in 1894, Tiomkin had been a concert pianist, an accompanist to silent films, and, following the Revolution, a champion of the work of Gershwin across Europe. He married Albertina Rasch, a noted Austrian ballerina-choreographer whose connections in Hollywood enabled her to recommend the inclusion of ballet sequences in the new sound musicals, and her husband's involvement in their accompaniment.

In the late 1930s Tiomkin's friendship with Capra led to his collaboration on *Lost Horizon* (1936), other major features, and the numerous wartime documentaries produced by Capra for the US government. *Only Angels Have Wings* (1939) was his first collaboration with Hawks, whilst *Shadow of a Doubt* (1943) marked the beginnings of his work with Hitchcock. Tiomkin's full-blown score for Vidor's epic *Duel in the Sun* (1946) established a relationship with the western that would continue through Hawks' *Red River* (1948) and *The Big Sky* (1952) to *High Noon* and later films. *High Noon*, in particular, was to create a vogue for theme songs which could be exploited by the post-war recording industry. In the course of a distinguished career he would rejoin Foreman in 1961 to provide the music for *The Guns of Navarone* and in 1969 to co-produce *MacKenna's Gold.*[9]

Gary Cooper

The most experienced figure to contribute to *High Noon* was of course its star, Gary Cooper, who had entered Hollywood as an extra in the 1920s and had made some 90 films by the time of his death in 1961. By the outbreak of WWII he was the highest-paid entertainer in America, a global cinematic icon associated with a powerfully solid and undemonstrative form of masc-uline performance. He was typically simple, thoughtful, moral, laconic and direct across three main kinds of role: the westerner, the soldier, and the ordinary joe. A run of successful vehicles appeared between 1940 and 1943 – Wyler's *The Westerner*, De Mille's *North-West Mounted Police*, Capra's *Meet John Doe*, Hawks' *Sergeant York* and *Ball of Fire*, Wood's *The Pride of the Yankees* and *For Whom the Bell Tolls* – the period in which Cooper won his only Oscar prior to *High Noon* (for *Sergeant York*). The later forties, however, were to prove a fallow

period for the star as he moved between variable roles and pictures. His box office value dropped as illness, age and marital unhappiness began to take their toll.[10]

High Noon was to be his eleventh post-war feature film. Eight of these films were for Warners, in a period when Cooper, like others, began to experiment with the possibilities of independence. In the first half of the post-war decade, Cooper made three war films (Lang's *Cloak and Dagger*, 1947, Daves' *Task Force*, 1949, and Hathaway's *You're In the Navy Now*, 1951), a social comedy (McCarey's *Good Sam*, 1948), and a romantic business drama (Curtiz' *Bright Leaf*, 1950). His most unusual social drama was Vidor's *The Fountainhead* (1948), from Ayn Rand's right-wing philosophical novel about the social role of the modern architect. In this period Cooper made only two westerns – De Mille's *Unconquered* (1947), with Paulette Goddard, and Heisler's *Dallas* (1950), with Ruth Roman.

Between 1951 and 1954, however, as he searched for a reliable dramatic format, five of the eight films he released revisited the western genre. Walsh's *Distant Drums* (1951) tells the story of the swamp fighters in the 1840s Seminole wars, while 1952 saw the release of *High Noon* and De Toth's *The Springfield Rifle*, a tale of Union counter-espionage in the Civil War. The two films of 1953 have interests in other kinds of social and geographic landscapes: Robson's *Return to Paradise* is a social parable in which Cooper plays a wanderer who helps to improve conditions on a Polynesian island, while Fregonese's *Blowing Wild* is a twentieth century oil-field drama set in Mexico. But the following year Mexico also provided the western setting for Hathaway's *Garden of Evil*, an adventure involving Red Indians and gold, and *Vera Cruz*, Aldrich's story of American adventurers caught up in the revolution of 1866. Of these films, just three deal with recent social and historical experience, specifically that of WWII, while the rest use Cooper to mediate narratives based on events or characters from the more distant history of the nineteenth century.

In *Cloak and Dagger* and *You're In the Navy Now* the expertise of civvy street is contrasted with the realities of military life. In *Cloak and Dagger* Cooper plays a physics professor caught up in special operations behind enemy lines, while in *You're In the Navy Now* his theoretical knowledge as an engineer is comically contrasted with the demands of life at sea. In *Task Force*, which dramatises the history of the aircraft carrier from the 1920s to Okinawa, Cooper is a more straightforward champion of the new technology against both the military hierarchy and the official enemy at large. Among the social dramas, *Bright Leaf* and *Blowing Wild* see Cooper coping with the rough-and-tumble of commercial life in the tobacco and oil industries, social settings which also feature strong romantic and emotional scenarios – love-triangles involving two women (*Bright Leaf*), and two men (*Blowing Wild*). Gentler fables about social values emerge in *Good Sam*, a Capra-esque story about a man who is generous to a fault, and *Return to Paradise*, a mythic story about wilderness and civilisation set on Samoa. *The Fountainhead* pursues the theme of male vision and integrity to anarchic and violent ends as Cooper's visionary architect Howard Roark dynamites a building rather than allow his original design to be compromised.

The westerns range from the low-cost simplicity of *High Noon* to the big-budget epic values of *Unconquered*. In the latter, Cooper plays the part of a loyal Virginian who, with the help of a young woman he has rescued from penal servitude, puts down an Indian rebellion fuelled by a fellow American. This structure is repeated in *Garden of Evil* and *Vera Cruz*, both dealing with the quest for gold (the 'black gold' of *Blowing Wild* is oil). In both films, Native Americans provide the larger enemy against which the foibles of whites can in turn be tested, and in both films the Cooper character is defined against other images of American masculinity (Widmark, Lancaster). The other westerns in this group, like *High Noon*, show the colonialists at war amongst themselves. The post Civil War drama *Dallas* is a vengeance western, in which, anticipating something of the structure of *High Noon*, Cooper tracks down the three men who have destroyed his family. As in *High Noon*, Cooper's wife is also separated from him in *The Springfield Rifle*, when, here posing as a traitor, he hides from her the true nature of his mission as he embarks on counterespionage. Incomplete if optimistic romantic scenarios are the norm in *Distant Drums*, *Garden of Evil*, and *Blowing Wild*.

Four further films of the period only featured minor contributions by Cooper, but are interesting for the extent to which they self-consciously play upon the audience's understanding of his star-image and his conventional generic affiliations. He appeared briefly as himself in Marshall's musical extravaganza *Variety Girl* (1947) and in Butler's story about Hollywood, *It's a Great Feeling* (1949), while his contributions to del Ruth's *Starlift* (1951) and the omnibus picture *It's a Big Country* (1951) gently parodied the western roles and ideologies with which he had come to be identified. These cameos reflect a period in which the values associated with the Cooper figure began to change and darken, and in which the character moved into middle age and isolation. *High Noon* is a more troubled work than most of his post-war films, matched only by *The Fountainhead* for its vision of individual isolation and determination, and then from a profoundly different political perspective. It was, however, to prove the film which restored critical and popular support long before the Oscars of 1953 by playing with and varying many of the historic features of the Cooper image.

One concrete measure of Cooper's changing popularity in the post-war years is provided by *Motion Picture Herald*'s annual 'Money-Making Stars Poll' of exhibitors. Cooper first crept into the bottom one or two places in the *MPH* polls in 1936 and 1937, but was always in the top 10 from 1941 to 1949. He reached number 2 in 1944, and held steady at number 4 from 1946 to 1948. He dropped out of this league altogether, however, in 1950, and only reappeared at number 8 in 1951, the year in which *High Noon* was made, when the list featured, in this order: John Wayne, Dean Martin/Jerry Lewis, Betty Grable, Abbott and Costello, Bing Crosby, Bob Hope, Randolph Scott, Doris Day and Spencer Tracy. But in 1952, the year of *High Noon*'s release, he rose to second place, and then, for the first time ever, he came top in 1953, the Oscar year for *High Noon*. Between 1954 and 1957, however, he slid slowly down the chart, dropping from the top ten permanently in 1958, three years before his death.[11]

An alternative measure is provided by *Variety*'s annual correlation of stars with box office revenues. In 1951, when *Dallas* only managed 34th position on $2.2m, Cooper did not feature among the top twenty box-office stars, who stretched from Gregory Peck ($11.75m) to Gordon MacRae ($4.4m). In 1952, when a smaller number of big box office successes reaped greater rewards, Cooper did not make a shortened list of just five stars: Robert Taylor ($20.23m), George Sanders ($17.5m), James Stewart ($16.75m), Charlton Heston and Cornel Wilde ($12m) and Gregory Peck ($9.5m). But Cooper's three films – *High Noon*, *Distant Drums* and *Springfield Rifle* – all figured in *Variety*'s annual top-grossing list (at nos. 8, 20 and 36 respectively) and their combined box office revenue ($8.65m) would certainly have put him among the top ten stars.[12]

Character Actors and New Faces

Key supporting roles were filled by a retinue of well-known character actors, who, like Cooper, generate countless intertextual memories. Behind Thomas Mitchell in his role as Jonas Henderson, the town elder who pragmatically and plausibly argues for Kane's departure, lie his Oscar-winning performance as Doc Boone in Ford's *Stagecoach* and his role as Scarlett's father in Fleming's *Gone With The Wind* (both 1939), whereas the disenchanted former sheriff Martin Howe is a far cry from Lon Chaney Jr.'s archetypal monster roles in 40s horror pictures. Otto Kruger, the suavely cynical Judge Percy Mettrick, had appeared in over thirty Hollywood roles following his days as a matinee idol in the 1920s. Including *High Noon* (in the role of Sam Fuller) and *My Six Convicts*, Henry Morgan made a total of four films in 1951, bringing his character parts up to 20 in ten years.

Other supporting actors had been more specifically associated with the character conventions of the western. After more than a dozen roles in the genre since 1941, Ian MacDonald's brief performance as the dreaded chief villain Frank Miller in *High Noon* provided him with one of his four western roles in 1951; he went on to play Geronimo in Sirk's *Taza, Son of Cochise* the following year, followed by parts in Ray's *Johnny Guitar* and Aldrich's *Apache* the year after. The role of Miller's henchman Pierce furnished Robert Wilke with one of the nearly sixty western roles he occupied since the late 1930s, while the self-interested and manipulative character of Deputy Harvey Pell provided Lloyd Bridges, an increasingly significant freelance actor after leaving Columbia in 1945, with his eighteenth western role since 1941. In 1955, Wilke, Bridges and Jack Elam (appearing in *High Noon* in a brief uncredited cameo) were again up against the town marshal in Tourneur's account of Wyatt Earp's urban clear-up, *Wichita*.

Kramer also introduced new players in *High Noon* – Roberta Haynes, Katy Jurado, Grace Kelly, Eve McVeagh, and Lee van Cleef. Haynes' role was eventually lost – she was to return to co-star with Cooper in *Return to Paradise* – and McVeagh's role as Mrs. Fuller is relatively minor, but the other newcomers were to make substantial contributions to the dramatic texture of *High Noon*. With over a dozen films to her credit, Jurado was a 'top cinema star south of the border', advised the *Hollywood Reporter*, and she would need no press agent since she was herself a film columnist for a range of Mexican publications. She appeared in Boetticher's *The Bullfighter and the Lady* in 1951 and, via Buñuel's *El Bruto* back in Mexico in 1952, went on to an Oscar nomination for her supporting role in Dmytryk's *Broken Lance* in 1954. Van Cleef, Kramer's only male discovery for *High Noon*, came to the film following a lengthy theatre run with Henry Fonda in *Mr. Roberts*. He would go on to be reincarnated as the villain of numerous Hollywood and spaghetti westerns.

But Kramer's major discovery was Grace Kelly. Arriving on Broadway in 1949 in a revival of Strindberg's *The Father* starring Raymond Massey, she had landed a bit part in Hathaway's *Fourteen Hours* two years later. A model, and an established star of TV soap opera, she came to *High Noon* in late August 1951 from summer stock in Denver. Zinnemann recalls seeking 'an attractive, virginal-looking and inhibited young actress, the typical western heroine', and Kelly fitted the role well 'perhaps because she was technically not quite ready for it, which made her rather tense and remote'. Tiomkin remembers her as 'an incongruous figure amid the crazy confusion' of the Motion Picture Center, where 'Nobody could foresee Princess Grace'. After an Oscar nomination for Ford's *Mogambo* (1953), she became a Hitchcock heroine in *Dial M for Murder* and *Rear Window* (both 1954) and the same year took the Oscar for best actress in Seaton's *The Country Girl*, yet another fifties film about marital disharmony.[13]

The interaction of these figures offers us an eminent case-study in the mechanics and dynamics of cinematic authorship at a crucial moment of change – institutional and industrial – in modern Hollywood cinema. It is a famous case which, surprisingly, has attracted little real analysis. Although many of the details are now sadly lost to us, those sources which remain available provide a working outline of the narrative of these decisive interactions. If there are a number of 'lives' behind and within and beyond *High Noon*, then the film, too, has a number of histories and identities. Its initial transformation from John Cunningham's short story into the interests of the Kramer company was completed in Foreman's shooting script, which, under the

direction of Fred Zinnemann, became the film itself in the period between Tuesday 5 September and the weekend of October 13-14 1951. It went into a lengthy and editorially complex post-production phase, the final version of the film being pre-viewed at the end of April 1952. Its popular career commenced at this point, leading up to the film's release at the end of July 1952, when, for a season, it was one of the most popular films in America. As its popularity waned over the winter of 1952, so its critical acclaim grew, and it accumulated a number of awards, culminating in the four Oscars it was awarded at the ceremony of March 1953.

2

. . . .

PRODUCT

Post-War Cinema

Even by the standards of an industry in seemingly perpetual flux, the early 1950s marked a period of particularly significant economic readjustment for Hollywood. At this stage, the golden years of large-scale popularity and profitability were coming to an end, and a steep decline was in view. A number of factors played their role in these changes. The monolithic industry was dramatically reorganised by the outcome of the 1948 Paramount decree, forcing the separation of the vertically-integrated studios and divorcing the business of production and exhibition. This anti-monopolistic legislation paved the way for a more complex industry in which new forms of independent production and exhibition would increasingly become the norm. This newly

Fred Zinnemann with Gary Cooper and Grace Kelly

competitive industry would be obliged to redefine itself in turn against the changing nature of post-war society. For its part, by 1950 the historic audience for cinema was undergoing massive change.[14]

Although incomes were, in overall terms, flat between 1946 and 1950, personal consumption rose dramatically as people cashed in the savings accumulated during wartime. Spending on consumer durables rose in line with a huge increase in housing build as American cities experienced an unprecedented exodus towards the developing suburbs. A 50% increase in home ownership was seen between 1945 and 1950, and, with it, a corresponding increase in marriages and the subsequent baby boom. Housing, consumer durables, and children took the place of the movies – now largely located in the downtown theatres at some distance from the new suburban growth. One important technological aspect of these trends was the arrival of domestic television, itself a key consumer durable. Television revenue of $0.5m in 1946 quadrupled annually to $34.3m in 1949 and then tripled to $106m in 1950. Further large increases took the totals from $236m in 1951 to $324m in 1953. By 1955 television was a true competitor with cinema and the most powerful symbol of American society's domestication of the audio-visual image.

Between 1935 and 1939 Hollywood released well over 700 films a year. This figure fell below 700 in 1940, and below 600 in 1941. It continued to fall into the low 400s by 1943-4, dipping below 400 in 1945 but then rising again into the upper 400s between 1946 and 1949. 1950 and 1951 were high years (622 and 654 respectively), but figures wavered again between the low 400s and low 500s between 1952 and 1954. In the boom year of 1946 United Artists' share was 20 releases, rising to 26 in 1947 and 1948 but falling back again to 21 and then 18 in 1949 and 1950. It effectively doubled these low totals in the years during which *High Noon* was made, released and celebrated at the Oscars (1951-3) – 46 (1951), 34 (1952) and 49 (1953). In the years of *High Noon*, 1651 pictures were released in total. *High Noon* would fulfil Kramer's last obligation to United Artists, the company which had released all the company's pictures since 1948, as he moved into his new expansionist relationship with Columbia. *High Noon* was thus one of the 34 films released by United Artists in 1952, and one of the 463 pictures released overall in that year. In the years of *High Noon*, over 300 westerns were released; it was one of the 108 westerns released in 1952.

The war years were a boom period for the Hollywood studios. 1946 was the peak year for studio profits, at around $120m. This was nearly double the 1945 figure, and double that for 1944 and 1943; nearly four times up on 1941, and six times that for 1939. While total US corporate profits grew, however, the film industry suffered major setbacks following 1946. It slumped by some 25% to a 1947 total of just over $87m, and was down by dramatic percentages to $30.8m in 1950. Although it held steady in 1951 at $31.1m, the years in which *High Noon* was released and celebrated were the low-points of the first half of the 1950s, at $23.9m and $22.8m respectively – just over one-sixth of the 'boom' total for 1946, only 5-6 years previously. Attendances declined rapidly in this period. Between 1930 and 1933 weekly cinema attendances in the US had dropped from 80m to 50m, climbing back to 84m ten years later, in 1943, but then dropping from 49m to 42m between 1951 and 1953; in 1952, 18,600 cinemas enjoyed weekly admissions of 43 million. At this stage the average had halved in ten years, and was running below the low-point of the Depression years. By 1959 the average had dropped below 40m (to 35m), dipping below 30m (to 27m) in 1961, and then below 20m (to 19m) in 1966.

As a result of this decline, the receipts of the US film industry dropped sharply. Between 1930 and 1940, US annual film receipts wavered between 0.5 and 0.7 billion dollars. In 1942 they rose above a billion dollars for the first time, climbing to $1692m in 1946 and then falling back to $1310m (1951), $1246 (1952), and $1187 (1953). Five years later, in 1958, they dipped below a billion, rising above that level only ten years later, in 1968. Since 1930, US box office receipts had hovered at around 1% of total consumer expenditure, reaching high-points of 1.29% and 1.24% in 1943 and 1944 respectively. In 1947 the percentage dropped below 1.0% for the first time since 1939, falling to 0.72% in 1950 and then, in 1951-3, to 0.64%, 0.57% and 0.52%, the latter figuring recurring until 1957, when it dropped again to 0.4%. The picture is not dissimilar for box office receipts expressed as a percentage of recreational expenditure – highs of 25.7% and 24.7% in 1943 and 1944, going down to 11.3%, 10.3%, and 9.3% in the years of *High Noon*.

In line with the industry in general, 1946 was a good year for United Artists, with record revenues of $37m, although at this level it was easily the smallest of the major studios. Columbia made $46.5m, and

Universal $53.9m, but the big five – Fox, MGM, Paramount, Warner Bros. and RKO – ranged from $120m to $190m. United Artists' profits were the smallest, at $0.4m, in a field led by Paramount on $39.2m. By 1950 United Artists revenues had slipped as low as an estimated $21.4m, a year in which a third annual loss was reported, this time of $1m. The years of *High Noon* were, by contrast, years of growth in revenues and profitability. A final slump in revenues to $19.6m in 1951 yielded, nonetheless, a profit of $0.3m, and, following reorganisation of the company early in that year, improvements to $29m and then $38.5m in 1952 and 1953 respectively showed profits rising to $0.4m and $0.6m for those years. From a 4% share of the movie market in 1949, United Artists had taken 10% by 1956.

Valuable films in the 1940s included Hughes' *The Outlaw* (1943) and Hitchcock's *Spellbound* (1945), together with Robson's *Home of the Brave* and *Champion* (both 1949). In the early 1950s, Gordon's *Cyrano de Bergerac* (1950) and Zinnemann's *High Noon* (1952) did well, along with Huston's *The African Queen* (1951) and *Moulin Rouge* (1952). Preminger's *The Moon is Blue* (1953), Aldrich's *Vera Cruz* (1954) and Kramer's *Not as a Stranger* (1955) were successful in the first half of the decade. Key directors of the decade were Kramer (eight films), Aldrich (six), Huston (five) and Kubrick (three). Seven of United Artists' 37 Oscars were garnered in 1952, four of them by *High Noon*. By this stage, the overall market was shrinking. United Artists remained stable at the bottom, although its profitability improved a little, largely thanks to the success of *High Noon*. At the top end, although MGM remained stable at $166.1m, its profits had dropped from 18% to 4.5%. Of the remaining companies, Columbia and Universal saw increased revenues of around one-third, but large reductions in profits. Paramount, Fox and Warner Brothers saw massive losses in revenue of between 40-50%, and reductions in profitability of down to a quarter and less.[15]

Preparing High Noon

Although *High Noon* did not go into production until the Autumn of 1951, Kramer and Foreman had expressed an earlier interest in the title and the theme. In 1948, while Foreman was working on the script of *Champion*, Kramer's company was approached by a representative of the United Nations who was canvassing film-makers about a possible film about the UN. Intrigued, Foreman began to consider an oblique approach to the subject through the vehicle of the western. His three-page outline of 1948 contained the bare bones of the eventual film. The marshal was named Will Tyler, the chief villain was Clyde Doyle, and his two cohorts were both his brothers. Helen Ramirez did not appear. Foreman's agent, E. Henry Lewis, found the story familiar, and John Cunningham's 1947 short story 'The Tin Star' was traced. It is not clear whether Foreman had read the story, but he accepted that he may well have done, and that he had perhaps been guilty of unconscious plagiarism. This story was to have various relationships, narrative and economic, to the future film.[16]

In March 1949 the title 'High Noon' was revealed to have been a strategic cover used by Kramer for his speedy and secretive production of *Home of the Brave* – written by Foreman, directed by Mark Robson, and scored by Dimitri Tiomkin – one of a group of controversial films about black issues that included Brown's *Intruder in the Dust*, Werker's *Boundaries*, Kazan's *Pinky* and Mankiewicz's *No Way Out*. In April, however, it was used for the first time to refer to the eventual western, when the *New York Times* reported a forthcoming 'western suspense yarn' which Mark Robson might add to his directorial credits for Kramer. By May, the spirit and practice of independent production epitomised for Kramer by *Home of the Brave* was directly linked to his ongoing plans for the 'real' *High Noon*, a film with 'a western background' which would tell 'the story of a town which died because it lacked sufficient fibre of citizenship to stand behind a man on moral grounds'.[17]

The film eventually materialised some two years later. In early 1951, Foreman created a fuller outline. Ben Maddow, too, reports working on a 'very rough, tentative version' of the film before being fired by Kramer on political grounds. Kramer would produce, but Foreman would take his first credit as Associate Producer. Recreating the partnership which had been responsible for *The Men*, Zinnemann, fresh from *Teresa* and engaged in negotiations to direct the first film in Cinerama, was signed to direct. It was a task for which Foreman himself, Mark Robson and Kramer's new signing Joseph Losey had been under consideration. Casting was jointly agreed by Kramer and Foreman, with Zinnemann's choices accepted where possible and his veto honoured. According to Zinnemann, it was 'a slow, difficult job of building up a fully-fledged film' from Cunningham's short story. While Foreman was 'struggling' with the first draft of the screenplay, the director himself had time to make *Benjy*, a fund-raising documentary short for the Los Angeles Orthopaedic Hospital, which went on to win an Oscar for Best Short. In the same period, Zinnemann and Clem Beauchamp were scouting locations and 'auditioning' railroad tracks all over the South-West. They found an ideal spot on the Santa Fe line near Gallup in New Mexico, but it proved too expensive. The historic Mother Lode area of Sonora was eventually chosen, some 300 miles north-east of Los Angeles.[18]

The gold-rush town of Columbia would provide the main town areas of Hadleyville, nearby Tuolumne City would provide the livery stable and church, while the water-tower at Warnerville, one of the last stops on the narrow-gauge Sierra Railroad, complete with its preserved wood-burning locomotive, would stand in as the Hadleyville railway station. Other external material would be shot at the Iverson ranch in Los Angeles. On 12 July, however, a further trip to Columbia revealed that the many trees on the main street were now in full leaf, thus interfering with the visualisation of the film; as a result, it was arranged to shoot these elements on the standing western street at the Columbia 'ranch' in the back-lot at Burbank, close to Warner Bros. The Warners studio can be seen in the upper portion of the famous shot – made with a camera-crane borrowed from George Stevens, who was shooting *Shane* next door – depicting the isolation of the marshall, a location which was to reappear as a Hawaiian street in *From Here to Eternity*.

'Believability' and 'excitement' were the qualities sought by the production team as they prepared the film, Zinnemann explained in 1952 when illustrating the 'choreography' of the final gunfight. Three stages of preparation were involved. Foreman's development of the sequence was discussed in detail with Kramer, Zinnemann, and the art director Rudolph Sternad. Zinnemann and the Art Department then worked out a 'routine', a series of thumbnail sketches which showed the shots needed and their interrelationships. After further meetings involving the cinematographer Floyd Crosby and the composer Dimitri Tiomkin – who made 'an extraordinary contribution' – the sketches were finalised and used as the 'pattern' for shooting. As a result, following the familiar Kramer method, actual production time and costs were reduced considerably.[19]

Clocks and railroad as symbolic icons in *High Noon*

3 4   The lonely marshal and the manhunt

Zinnemann visualised the film around three elements: the atmosphere of threat hanging over the film, symbolised by 'the motionless railroad tracks, always static'; the victim, 'looking for help, in constant movement, black against the white sky'; and the urgency of 'time perceived as an enemy, shown by obsessive use of clocks ... looming larger as time slips by, pendulums moving more and more slowly until time finally stands still, gradually creating an unreal, dreamlike, almost hypnotic effect of suspended animation'.[20] Disappointingly for Zinnemann, one memorable time-piece did not find its way into the film: one without numbers or hands, of the kind he had seen outside Utter-McKinley's mortuary on Sunset Strip. The film would be shot in black-and-white, like nearly 80% of films that year, and in a standard aspect ratio; cinemascope would arrive just as *High Noon* took its Oscars, in March 1953. With Crosby, Zinnemann chose to adopt a 'newsreel' style for the film, based on the Civil War photographs of Matthew Brady and assisted by the smog of Burbank. Resisting pressure to revert to a more traditional style, Crosby refused filters, soft focus and spotlights in an attempt to reproduce 'the flat light, the grainy textures, the white sky' of Brady's imagery.[21]

Production
With primary finance amounting to some $200,000 secured from Bruce Church, a California lettuce grower who had backed *The Men* and *Cyrano*, *High Noon* was budgeted at $794,000. This would have been higher than *Champion* and *Home of the Brave*, at $500,000 each, but substantially less than *So This is New York*, which had cost around $1m. It would have been lower than the average cost for a feature film in 1951, which, according to the *Motion Picture and Television Almanac*, stood at $900,000. In mid-July, the *Hollywood Reporter* was able to announce the signing of Cooper as lead, a role with which the names of Kirk Douglas, Marlon Brando, Montgomery Clift and Charlton Heston had been linked. It was one for which Foreman himself had considered Henry Fonda, and one rejected by Gregory Peck because it came too close to King's *The Gunfighter* (1950). Church insisted on Cooper, who dropped his asking fee of $275,000 to $60,000 plus a percentage of the profits in a 'participation' deal of the kind that had been so successful for Jimmy Stewart.[22]

The assignment of key production personnel (cinematographer Floyd Crosby, designer Percy Ikerd, sound engineer Jean Speak, composer Dimitri Tiomkin, designer Ralph Sternad) followed during August, along with the signing of further players, a process of recruitment which was to continue well into the production period itself. Grace Kelly was given less than three weeks' confirmation of her involvement in a film for which 'High Noon'was even then only a provisional title, summoned by telegram on 10 August to be ready for the first day of rehearsal on 28 August. This was a hectic period for Kramer, with five films in production – something of a record for an independent producer – three of them involving location work. *Death of a Salesman* started first, on 20 August, a week before *High Noon*; *The Four Poster* started three weeks later, on 11 September; *My Six Convicts* began rehearsal on 17 September and was on location in San Quentin a week later; *The Sniper*, shooting in San Francisco, started a week further on. A month after the start of *High Noon*, Kramer was able to announce his *coup* in acquiring the rights to the biography of Roosevelt, along with Elinor's agreement to participate as an advisor. Foreman recalls being left alone in a close and productive relationship with Zinnemann on a project for which Kramer had little time and in which he reportedly showed little interest.[23]

A one-week rehearsal period started with a pep talk by Kramer on Tuesday 28 August. Cooper, surprisingly, and in excess of the terms of his contract, insisted on joining in. Commencing 5 September, *High Noon* was one of three dozen Hollywood pictures in production on that date. It ran for twenty-eight days until the weekend of 13-14 October. Within a week of the start of production, Kramer was introducing his stars to the American public through the new medium of television. The four-week shoot, including the location work at Sonora, was efficient if tense. Its stars were undergoing their own personal anxieties and tensions. It was easy for Cooper to comply with Zinnemann's instruction to look 'tired', as he was troubled by arthritis, back pain, and an ulcer. An operation in July was to be followed, after shooting ended, by the discovery that a further operation was needed for a hernia. Unhappily separated from his wife Rocky, he was not entirely secure in an affair with Patricia Neal. Chaperoned by her youngest sister, Lizanne, Grace Kelly remained tense and introspective as she embarked on her first major film role. There were also wider institutional pressures affecting the production. For all the apparent generic familiarity of *High Noon*, the approach adopted by the Kramer team met with puzzlement and resistance: an ageing male star paired with a much younger leading lady, unknown female leads, an experimental visual style, and, moreover, a conspicuous leftist at the helm.

Foreman and HUAC

The reentry of HUAC into Hollywood in 1951 had one again raised the political temperature. From March onwards, the Committee linked such figures as Judy Holliday, José Ferrer, Marlon Brando and Lee J. Cobb with Communist front organisations; Howard da Silva, Gale Sondergard, Waldo Salt, Paul Jarrico and Abraham Polonsky were unfriendly witnesses. Edward Dmytryk, Sterling Hayden, Robert Rossen and Budd Schulberg named names. Foreman's struggle with the screenplay was overdetermined by the difficulties of his own political position from the Spring of 1951 onwards. He received his subpoena in April; the hearings, planned for June, were delayed until September. In the middle of work on *High Noon*, Foreman turned on the TV one morning to hear himself named, among many others, by Martin Berkeley. He finally appeared on 24 September, along with writer and associate producer Lester Koenig and story editor Donald Gordon. Refusing to answer questions, he pleaded instead a variation of the Fifth Amendment dubbed the 'diminished' Fifth.[24]

Foreman had not known how Kramer would react to news of the subpoena, but received his early support. He was particularly anxious to keep Cooper informed. The latter offered to appear before the Committee on Foreman's behalf and secured agreement for Foreman's intended position from his friend Bruce Church, the primary backer. Cooper went on to support Foreman publicly when Foreman explained the position to the crew of *High Noon*. Kramer, for his part, broke with Foreman immediately following the hearings: Foreman saw Kramer's refusal to discuss matters with him in person as 'the ultimate betrayal'. A final settlement took place just a week after the completion of production on *High Noon*. Foreman's lawyer Stanley Cohn was left to negotiate with Sam Zagon, pushing the price of Foreman's buy-out from the company up from the $55,000 on offer to an acceptable $250,000. The situation with *High Noon* itself was critical to these negotiations: it transpired that, having purchased the Cunningham rights himself for $1,500, Foreman had never officially assigned them over to the company.[25]

A public offensive ensued, led by John Wayne, president of the right-wing Motion Picture Alliance for the Preservation of American Ideals, and influential columnist Hedda Hopper. Foreman's publicist Henry Rogers was assailed by a barrage of angry and threatening phone calls from Wayne, Ginger Rogers, Ward Bond, and other MPAPAI members. Zinnemann and Cooper remained loyal to Foreman. Cooper, for all his conservatism, was recalled by Foreman as the only major figure to offer support until he, too, bowed to threats from Louis B. Mayer and Walter Wanger concerning his future employment prospects. Within ten days Cooper had diplomatically and courteously withdrawn from Foreman's proposed new company.[26]

Wayne's hostility to *High Noon* continued unabated for many years. Like Lloyd Bridges (who had given secret testimony to the Committee), he initially attempted to persuade Foreman to cooperate and to name names. Presenting Cooper with his Oscar for *High Noon* in 1953, he chose, curiously, to express his professional envy of Cooper's good luck in working with the kind of writer who could produce such a splendid role for him. Wayne continued to inveigh against the film, however, long after his own starring role in *Rio Bravo*, Howard Hawks' retort to *High Noon*. In the early seventies he told *Playboy* of his continuing pleasure in having helped expel Foreman from America, and, while filming Hickox's *Brannigan* (1975) in Britain, he continued the assault in an appearance on TV's *Michael Parkinson Show*, triggering a powerfully satirical response from Foreman in *Punch*.[27]

But Foreman was not the only victim associated with Kramer and *High Noon*. Losey was also disengaged by Kramer for political reasons, and, like Foreman, headed for an uncertain future in England. An unsung victim of the period, veteran character actor Howland Chamberlin – the foxy hotel clerk who tells Amy he wouldn't miss the showdown between Miller and the marshall 'for all the tea in China' – was also blacklisted, re-surfacing a quarter of a century later in Benton's *Kramer vs Kramer* (1979). His period on *High Noon* was poignantly recalled by Foreman. In the public sphere, however, Foreman's film, airbrushed of its politics, was already on its way to acquiring mythic status, heralded by the uncaptioned still of Cooper as Will Kane which filled a page of the *Hollywood Reporter* in the last week of October and would provide a potent icon for film exhibitors seeking a telling narrative image for the film.[28]

Post-Production

The drama and the mystery of *High Noon*, however, were not yet over, for the post-production history of the film is still a further major source of professional controversy. Precisely what transpired between October 1951 and its first official preview nearly six months later has been very differently described by its producer, its director, and one of its editors, Elmo Williams. How the film looked, for example, towards the end of October 1951, after Zinnemann and Williams had spent a week or ten days on a rough cut, is not entirely clear. Part of the debate centres on what Zinnemann refers to as a 'protection' sequence involving a brief sub-plot in which a second deputy dallies at a Mexican staging-post outside town. The fate of this sub-plot is something of a mystery. According to Zinnemann, only two or three shots were filmed, and he abandoned the sub-plot with relief, since it would have destroyed the unity of time and place for which he was aiming. The material in question, which had been saved for the last two days of location shooting at Sonora, turned out to be disappointing: the weather broke, the work was rushed, and the fight scene proved difficult to stage. According to other accounts, however, the final version of the film may be substantially shorter following the removal of this material at a later stage of editing.[29]

Williams recalls productive exchanges with the director, and the strengthening of the film. But he also recalls that the rough-cut disappointed Kramer, and, fearing his replacement by another editor, Williams sought permission for another attempt at the material while Kramer was away. He eliminated the 'protection' material, increasing the emphasis on Kane and his problems by tightening some of the material between Amy and Helen, as well as a scene between Helen and Harvey Pell. Williams showed a further rough-cut to Kramer upon his return, playing him a Burl Ives recording of 'Riders in the Sky' over the silent prologue to suggest a possible musical dimension. Kramer welcomed the changes, and accepted the musical suggestion, going on to commission Tiomkin, who had been involved since pre-production, to provide a song-based score. According to the composer, *High Noon* was regarded at this stage as 'the ugliest duckling of all ... a real stinkeroo'. Kramer's own account is different again. He claims credit for definitive editorial work at later stages. Kramer recalls working at Columbia during the week, editing *High Noon* at night and at weekends at another independent studio. Following further work on sound and narrative, an unsuccessful public preview suggested that the sub-plot – the material Williams claims to have eliminated at an early post-Zinnemann phase – was extraneous and that the musical *leitmotif* was now overdone, the audience responding with laughter as the song became repetitive. The sub-plot was therefore removed, as were some repetitions of the song, shortening the film, he claims, by up to fifteen minutes.

If it seems unlikely that we will now be able to confirm the full chronology of the various stages in the evolution of the final version of the film, what is certain is that in the period between mid-October 1951 and the film's eventual official preview on 28 April 1952, Tiomkin took a further musical initiative which had far-reaching consequences not only for *High Noon* but for the wider synergy between the cinema and the rapidly evolving music industry. When Ritter's record company did not express an interest, he went ahead to release a version of the song with Frankie Laine, for Columbia, in early summer 1952. Ritter followed suit for Capitol, and Bill Hayes joined the fray for MGM, giving the song triple exposure in the run-up to the film's release at the end of July. All three versions did well, but Ritter, with his now historically distanced cowboy persona, was up against a sweeter and more 'modern' version by Laine, complete with female chorus, a new star following the success of his 1951 smash hit 'Jealousy'.

Laine's 'Do Not Forsake Me' entered the overall *Variety* chart, as polled by top US disc jockeys, for the last-but-one week of July 1952. It jumped 25 places in a week, climbed to equal 11th within a month, and peaked at number 7 for a fortnight in September. It then see-sawed up and down during October and early November, disappearing from the ranking in the middle of the month. It became one of the top 40 retail discs of the year, entering the sales chart at number 15 in early July 1952; reaching the top 10 in the first week of August, where it remained until the end of October; and slipping out of the top 20 by the end of the month. It was one of the top 10 jukebox songs from early September to late October, and from July to November the song was always among the top 50 songs on radio, two-thirds of the time in the top 30. But Ritter was not totally eclipsed: on Oscar night, he would once more sing the 'authentic' version, inaugurating a lengthy personal association with the ceremony.[30]

Exhibition and Reception

High Noon was supported by a wave of strong reviews following the April 1952 preview, although none of these could foresee its impact on the market later in the summer.[31] Supported by a careful build-up in the trade, distribution deals were signed in June for a late summer release, a growing phenomenon which differed sharply from the time-honoured delay until Labour Day. The experience of wartime patterns of attendance, the new technology of air-conditioning, and the fallow period for the new medium of television now recommended the summer months as a potentially lucrative period for film exhibition. In 1952 specifically, a break in the record 13-day heatwave helped strengthen attendances, even

in competition with the televising of the Democratic convention in Chicago. *High Noon* was one of the six new films opening in the third week of July at the Mayfair cinema in New York, where it ran for two months. There it followed Sirk's social comedy about wealth and social class *Has Anybody Seen My Gal?*, starring James Coburn, Piper Laurie, Rock Hudson, and James Dean, and was eventually succeeded by Walsh's *The World in His Arms*, a romantic melodrama with Gregory Peck, Ann Blyth, and Anthony Quinn. *High Noon* was accompanied throughout by the short *Bug Parade*, coupled at first with *Future Generals* and then with *Ski-lark in the Rockies*. At the 1,736 seat-Mayfair, *High Noon* was the third big newcomer ($44,000) in New York, even if a long way behind Taurog's farce with Dean Martin and Jerry Lewis, *Jumping Jacks* ($117,000) and Binyon's comedy with Clifton Webb and

Male potency at stake in an advertisement launching *High Noon* on the US West Coast

Ginger Rogers, *Dreamboat* ($105,000). Together, these three films accounted for half the week's estimated take of $521,000 from eighteen Broadway cinemas.[32]

Key city grosses, according to *Variety*, amounted to $2,186,700 from 197 theatres across 23 cities, chiefly first runs, including New York. *High Noon* played its part in this, with six openings which together accumulated just over twice the New York total. Personal appearances by Kelly and Jurado helped the 2,360-seat Boyd in Philadelphia to a 'lofty' $24,000. At the 1,500-seat Astor in Boston it soared 'way over' advance hopes with $17,000. At Portland's 1,850-seat Liberty, the lack of air-conditioning did not prevent the film from taking $15,000. In Pittsburgh, the 2,200-seat Harris took $13,000, its 'heftiest' receipts of the year. At the 2,300-seat State Cinema in Minneapolis, the film made $12,000. Its overall total of $134,000 represented approximately one-sixteenth of the key city gross total for the week in question. *High Noon* was the only newcomer in *Motion Picture Herald*'s 'Box Office Champions' for August 1952, a list of five or six titles based on gross revenue at key city theatres throughout the country. *High Noon*'s stablemates in August were *The Greatest Show on Earth*, De Mille's Big Top epic on its way to the Best Picture Oscar and in its third month of championship, together with *Jumping Jacks*; LeRoy's musical *Lovely to Look At*, Annakin's *The Story of Robin Hood*, and Curtiz's biopic, *The Story of Will Rogers*, starring the comedian's son – all listed for a second month.[33]

Variety confirmed some of these titles, but with alternatives. Its top 12 for August 1952, based on the reports from correspondents in some 25 cities, started with *High Noon* itself, giving United Artists its biggest earner since *The African Queen*. *Jumping Jacks* appeared second, down from its top place in July, but only pipped to the post by *High Noon* by virtue of being mainly in holdover or because it had played out most of its principal key dates; *The Greatest Show on Earth* came in at number 8; *Lovely to Look At* appeared ninth; *The Story of Robin Hood* at number 10. *The Story of Will Rogers*, however, did not appear at all in the *Variety* list, which instead ranked from third to seventh such films as Sherman's *Affair in Trinidad*, Walsh's *The World in His Arms*, Baker's *Don't Bother to Knock*, Butler's *Where's Charley?*, and Binyon's *Dreamboat*. Of these twelve, according to *Variety*, there was very close competition between *High Noon*, *Jumping Jacks*, *Affair in Trinidad*, and *The World in His Arms*, each taking a week in turn in the number one position.[34]

The film recouped $2.5 million in 18 weeks, making it the fastest liquidating film in the history of United Artists, and the prime reason for the company's modest profitability in 1952.[35] An impression of the breadth of its success can be gleaned from *Motion Picture Herald*'s 'Independent Film Buyers' Report on Performance', in which it appeared for eighteen weeks from its release. This weekly table listed over 100 current films, and over 4,000 engagements, scoring films on a five-point scale. *High Noon*'s engagements rose steadily from seven in August to 68 by the end of 1952 as its qualities were recognised by audiences and by exhibitors. Its initial two scores of 'excellent' rose to five for the second and third entries, and then to seven for the remainder of the period. 'Above average' scores rose from five to a final total of 33; an 'average' of 2 was scored on the second entry, which was constant for several entries, eventually rising to 13. The film never recorded a 'below average' or 'poor'. In *Variety*'s overall listing of 'Top Grossers of 1952', *High Noon* appeared at Number 8. The top dozen took between $12m (*The Greatest Show on Earth*) and $3.2m (*The Quiet Man*). Ahead of *High Noon* (on $3.4m) were *The Greatest Show* , LeRoy's *Quo Vadis*, Thorpe's *Ivanhoe*, King's *The Snows of Kilimanjaro*, Walker's *Sailor Beware*, *The African Queen*, and *Jumping Jacks*.[36]

High Noon began to add critical acclaim to box office success with a series of awards in the first quarter of 1953. The New York Film Critics Award led to a return run in Hollywood in January, and in the same month it won awards from *Photoplay* and was nominated for the Oscars and the Screenwriters Guild award. It won the *Look* magazine award towards the end of the month, and, within the first three weeks of March, a Golden Globe, a Screenwriters Guild award and a clutch of Oscars. However, all was not plain sailing. Amid continuing political tension the Screenwriters Guild was attacked for its award to Foreman in a vituperative front-page item by the editor of the *Hollywood Reporter*.[37] Reclaiming the film for the western genre, the city of Reno, Nevada, awarded it their Silver Spurs award for the best Western of the year. At the main event in their three-day festival in May, Montgomery Clift stood in for Gary Cooper, while, as Zinnemann recalls, the master of ceremonies was 'a youngish leading man from Warner Brothers by the name of Ronald Reagan',[38] who, as president of the Screen Actors Guild, had complimented Sterling Hayden on his performance at the Spring 1951 HUAC hearings.

Although the *Variety* straw poll strongly tipped *High Noon* for Best Picture at the Oscars of March 1953, De Mille's *The Greatest Show on Earth* unexpectedly carried off the prize on its way to becoming one of the biggest money spinners of the post-war years. *The Greatest Show* presents a different – and a cruder – fable about human triumph against overwhelming odds, and about the contestation between men and women, through the emblem of the circus rather than the western outpost. Its victory symbolised a different preference in another sense: its director had been the arch conservative against whom the liberals had ranged themselves in the battle over the loyalty oath in the Directors Guild in Autumn 1950. But there were still four prizes for *High Noon* in an awards ceremony rescued from financial difficulties by the new medium of television. Nominated five times since 1939, Gary Cooper took his first Academy Award since *Sergeant York* and became the first actor to win an Oscar for a western role since Warner Baxter's Cisco Kid in Walsh's *In Old Arizona* at the second Awards ceremony for 1928-29. Harry Gerstad and Elmo Williams won the Oscar for Best Editing, while Dimitri Tiomkin enjoyed a double triumph, with Oscars for Best Score, and, with Ned Washington, for Best Song. Zinnemann was nominated

The circus as a metaphor for social cohesion following the train crash in De Mille's *The Greatest Show on Earth* for Best Director, but would have to wait another year for such an honour with *From Here to Eternity*; on this occasion the honours went to John Ford for *The Quiet Man*. Carl Foreman, nominated but unsuccessful, studied the TV screen with some emotion as his early mentor Dore Schary presented the Oscar for Best Screenplay to Charles Schnee for Minnelli's *The Bad and the Beautiful*.

Seen in the longer historical term, *High Noon* is a medium/high earner where rental incomes are concerned, understood either in specific genre terms or in relation to the feature film in general. *High Noon* did not secure a place in *Variety*'s 1990 list of 'all-time Western rental champs', which included films which had secured rentals (i.e. distributors' receipts, not ticket sales) in the US and Canada of over $4m. The calculations did not include inflation, nor any non-theatrical revenues, which could affect figures dramatically. Ninety films figured in such a list, peaking with Brooks' *Blazing Saddles* (1974) and Hill's *Butch Cassidy and the Sundance Kid* (1969) at $47.8m and $46.04m respectively, followed some way behind by Laughlin's *Billy Jack* (1971) and Pollack's *The Electric Horseman* (1979) at $31.10m and $30.28m respectively, with a further drop to Pollack's *Jeremiah Johnson* (1972) at $21.90m and then close competition all the way down the remaining 85 titles. An alternative approach, with an allowance for inflation built into the calculation, naturally produced a higher set of figures all round. The lowest of 50 entries in such a study was Peckinpah's *The Wild Bunch* (1969), slightly lower than in *Variety*'s chart, but worth $10.6m as opposed to *Variety*'s $5.3m, rising to *Duel in the Sun*, adjusted up from $19m to $70m and leaping from eighteenth to first place as a result, followed by *Butch Cassidy* and *Blazing Saddles*, down from first and second in the *Variety* chart, with $58.4m and $49.2m respectively. In this list, *High Noon* entered at number 34, with rentals of $3.4m adjusted up to $18.7m.[39]

3
. . . .
TEXT

Characters, Relations
High Noon has three main storylines. One is the story of the relationship between Will Kane and Frank Miller, a story in which the past erupts into

the present and which results in a fearful re-enactment of an ancient drama. The second, triggered by the first, is the story of the interrupted marriage of Will Kane and Amy Foster, when Kane's commitment to a final confrontation with Miller obliges Amy to leave him in defence of her Quaker principles. The third triangulates with the first two. It is the story of Kane's relations with a series of townsfolk – and, in certain cases, their negotiations with each other – to support him in his struggle against Miller. It is her encounter with one of the townsfolk, Helen Ramirez, which finally re-ties these stories together as Amy turns back to rejoin her husband and becomes his only 'deputy' in the final shoot-out.

The story thus deals with the processes and rituals of social formation and de-formation. The opening rituals are forward-moving and positive: Kane marries Amy, and retires as marshall, in a scene which brings together marriage and the law in the kiss Kane extracts from Amy as the 'pay' for the relinquishment of his legal duties. His attempt to reverse the flow, however, is unsuccessful. When he insists on returning to the town and to his job, Amy is obliged to regard this as a dereliction of their marriage; the townsfolk, for their part, cannot for various reasons accept Kane back into an identity which throws their own new-found harmony and stability into further crisis. Kane's task across the film is to steer a lonely path through his abandonment by Amy and by the townsfolk. Only one side of the equation can be restored, as Amy is won over by reading the copy of the last will and testament she finds in Kane's office. The film concludes with a technical symmetry by repeating Kane's and Amy's departure from the town, but their departure on this occasion signifies a real separation from the values of the town and townsfolk.

This classic structure involves a story about the law accompanied and overlaid by a story of the heterosexual couple; activity focussed around a central heroic figure; a strong linear movement governed by a very specific programme of time; a climax in which physical interaction resolves a tension which has hitherto been characterised by dialogue and inaction. Intent upon preserving the unities of space and time, the film proceeds as a chamber drama, in which key encounters take place in closed interiors as characters anticipate the impact of Miller's journey into Hadleyville. The actions which connect these waiting characters and these confined spaces are of two kinds, walks and looks. Kane's world becomes that of the street, as he goes on a series of walks – in the script, Zinnemann referred to them as 'plods' – around the town. Much of the narrative shape of the film depends upon the tension of these walks in the Sunday morning heat, the understated nature of the negotiations, and Will's uncomplaining recognition that the world he is exploring is shrinking all around him.

Negotiations, Looks, the Hero

Gary Cooper's Will Kane appears in nearly half the main scenes of the film and these take up three-quarters of the running time. His work as hero is that of negotiation: he spends much of the film approaching possible helpers, seeking help and also rejecting it. In as many as seventeen key scenes, he discusses his situation and his needs with characters who either mark their difference from him, or unsuccessfully attempt to deny difference altogether (the drunk, Jimmy, and the boy, Johnny, are gently but firmly placed back into their own realities). Judge Mettrick packs his bags, reminding Kane of similar reversals of fortune which befell both Athens in the Fifth Century BC and the town of Indian Falls within the last decade: 'Look, this is just a dirty little village in the middle of nowhere. Nothing that happens here is really important … Get out!'. The price of Harvey Pell's support is Kane's endorsement of his ambition to become the new marshall; Kane refuses. The assembled saloon turns down Kane's appeal for deputies. Sam Fuller hides from Kane and gets his wife to tell Kane he is in church. Kane's predecessor and long-term friend Mart Howe has broken knuckles and is arthritic; he would hinder, not help, and he is in any case bitter: 'You risk your skin catching killers and the juries let them go so they can come back and shoot at you again. If you're honest, you're poor your whole life, and in the end you wind up dying all alone in a dirty street. For what? For nothing. A tin star.'

The moral centre of the film is the scene in the church when Kane goes to appeal for help. The first contribution is provided by the minister who, starting to read a text from *Malachi* IV predicting the fate of the 'proud' and 'wicked' in the day that will burn 'as an oven', reproaches Kane for his lack of commitment to the church. Early expressions of support are interrupted by reminders that Kane is no longer actually the marshal, and that there is 'personal trouble' between himself and Miller. Coy blames the politicians 'up north' for releasing Miller; Sawyer wants

Kane's interiority

The wedding look

to know why, having paid 'good money' for law officers, the townsfolk are now being asked to do the job themselves; another has argued for more deputies all along; Ezra, ashamed of what he has been hearing, supports 'the best marshal this town ever had', and warns of future trouble unless he is supported now. A further contributor wonders if Miller is even on the train, whilst the minister cannot bring himself to urge members of his flock to break the Commandment against killing. In the longest and conclusive contribution, Henderson turns a long circle. The problem is their own, that of the people who have built the town 'from nothing'. But people 'up north' have been contemplating investment in Hadleyville, 'to put up stores, build factories', and news of mayhem on the streets would set the town back five years. He wishes that Kane had not bravely returned, because without him, he feels there would be no trouble. Tomorrow, under a new marshal, and with their support, he thinks 'we can handle everything that comes along'. With that he urges Will to leave.

Once Judge Mettrick has departed from Hadleyville early in the film, the only accompanying male figure associated with the law is Harvey Pell, who enters into a mental and emotional struggle with Kane over his failure to achieve promotion to marshal. He is threatened by the arrival of the new marshal much as Kane is threatened by the impending arrival of Frank Miller. He competes with Kane and with his lover Helen Ramirez, and is defeated by both. The expulsion of the false agent of the law, exposed as self-seeking and craven, is a major narrative drive which concludes with his departure from the story three-quarters of the way through the film. In both cases, physical contestation is involved; he loses an ambiguous fist-fight with Will and is slapped down by Helen in an exchange where she insists on her own control of her physical relations to men. As Kane's 'other', Harvey must be shown to be eventually 'unacceptable' to key men and women. In these exchanges, deep-seated ambiguities in the Cooper repertoire are opened up repeatedly. The man of action must endure passivity; his moral heroism compels a kind of stasis, since no real action can take place until noon. Will's passivity is in fact dictated by the action of another, that of Frank Miller; for Will himself to 'act' would mean absentation and defeat: his only option is to flee. His opportunity for self-expressive heroism is thus postponed, and in the meantime his possibility for action is reduced to the search for expressions of support and help (which do not

Preliminary struggles:
smoked out of the stables by the Miller gang, and resisting Harvey Pell

materialise). He is a 'seeker hero' whose reward is merely a kind of jaundiced social knowledge very different from the material solidarity he truly needs.

Whilst some of these exchanges are direct and transparent, others are marked as hypocritical and even venal. In these cases, Will's job is to simply watch and to discern the 'value' of the responses which he prompts. Since, by definition, he has no right to respond, and also no-one with whom to share the 'knowledge' which he thus acquires, the spectator's reading of Will's relations is intuitive and implicit, rather than explicit and hard-edged. Instead of identifying with our hero's actions, we identify with the chain of voiceless looks which mark his acceptances of rejection and denial. The hero's look in *High Noon* does not often, therefore, carry the active charge associated with the gender symbolism of the Hollywood text. Rather, it is the face of Gary Cooper as an index of his passivity and yet his perspicacity which is the key domain for the spectator in *High Noon*. This profoundly masochistic toning of the star image – deliberately emphasised in the editing, according to a Cooper biographer – may in fact correspond to long-term ambiguities in the 'gendering' of the star's image from the silent period onwards.[40]

Women: Type and Stereotype
Although the film is routinely understood as a drama about the isolation of Will Kane, he only appears in total isolation when he writes his will and testament late in the film. Tellingly, however, the bulk of this segment is taken up with the lengthy montage of other characters as the clock strikes twelve. For Kane's appearances are usually focused not on his isolation, but on negotiation or confrontation. Some twenty-seven segments, just over three-quarters of the total, feature subsidiary characters, and in nearly half these segments characters interact with each other in isolation from Kane. This focuses attention on the relationship between Harvey Pell and Helen Ramirez, between Helen and Amy Fowler/Kane, between Helen, Sam, and Mr. Weaver. We can say that the relationships thus privileged stress the female dimensions of the film, and the film's handling of ethnicity.

Whereas the continuity between marshal and deputy was one theme of 'The Tin Star', and women but an absent influence, in *High Noon* female characters are central to the drama. Like Harvey Pell,

Woman on the edge of revolt: Helen Ramirez

they get about half as many segments as the central character. Amy, for her part, is not the conventional Eastern school-teacher of the western genre. In Foreman's preface to the script, she is 'one of the new women of the period ... who are beginning to rebel against the limitations and restrictions of the Victorian epoch ... determined not to be a sheltered toy-wife but a full partner in her marriage, and it is she who has planned their future.' In the script itself, Amy had problems with her family: 'My family didn't want me to marry Will in the first place ... I seem to make them unhappy no matter what I do. Back home they think I'm very strange. I'm a feminist. You know, women's rights – things like that ...'. Her attitude to marriage is critical: 'What made him my man? A few words spoken by a Judge? Does that make a marriage? ... There's too much wrong between us – it doesn't fit! Anyway, this is what he chose ...'[41]

Helen Ramirez, equally, is more than the generic Latin stereotype. She is substantially described by Foreman, who is keen to place her in terms of nationality, social status, and personal history. Two or three years Kane's senior, she is 'a victim of an era and environment with rigid social standards. ... half Mexican, and thus neither acceptable to the 'pure' American women of the region, nor eligible for a 'good' marriage'. Consequently, 'in addition to being intelligent, shrewd and strong-willed, she is also hard and resentful. Physically, she is handsome, full-breasted, passionate. More, she has style, personality.' After the death of her husband Ramirez, the local saloon-keeper, she disposed of her interests in the saloon and became a silent partner in the town's general store. She has been sexually involved with Miller, Kane, and now Harvey Pell; she herself 'selected' Kane as Miller's successor, and she still cannot forgive Kane for ending the affair, since 'this is a privilege she reserves for herself'.[42]

Villainy

Whereas their target is alone, the villains of *High Noon*, in a familiar dramatic trope, are multiple. They include a strong familial dimension – the Miller brothers Ben and Frank, joining a long line of villainous fraternal broods stretching from the Clanton brothers in Ford's *My Darling Clementine* (1946) to the Hammonds in Peckinpah's *Ride the High Country* (1961). Once they have foregathered, they are inactive for the bulk of the film, unlike its hero, who is in constant motion as he seeks

Law and disorder: the judge abandons Hadleyville to the Miller gang

to build his own team. Although the chief villain Frank Miller is absent until the closing stages of the film, he is feared and must be finally confronted because, says Kane, he is 'crazy'. His supposed mania (predicted by other characters, but which does not in fact materialise) is anticipated by the demeanour of his brother Ben, who is headstrong (he has to be restrained on his arrival in town), has to be warned about his drinking (which leads him into an uneasy encounter with Kane at the saloon), and who embodies sexual threat. He takes an immediate interest in Amy ('*That* wasn't here five years ago') and it is the ominous announcement of Ben's sexual desire when he breaks a shop window to steal a woman's bonnet ('I just want to be ready') which alerts Kane to the gang's whereabouts in the final shoot-out.

The villains provide a rhythmic baseline for the film. They book-end the text, featuring strongly at the beginning and the end. In the centre of the film, there is an overall symmetry to their presence/absence. Between segments 14 and 21 they appear four times, leading to a balanced series of absences. On either side of this central passage they are absent for six segments in either direction. They thus have a structuring presence/absence which does not depend upon either action or extensive representation of any kind. Apart from the book-end segments their appearances are very brief – twice for less than a minute, on four occasions for less than thirty seconds. Their function is largely to wait, and to overcome their own internal friction as a group, in contrast with Kane's increasingly desperate attempts to form a coherent male unit to compete with them.

Time and Place

As far as Foreman was concerned, time and place were somewhat abstract in *High Noon*: 'THE TIME is about 1870 or 1875. THE PLACE IS HADLEVILLE [*sic*], population around 400, located in a Western territory still to be determined, a town just old enough to have become pleasantly aware of its existence, and to begin thinking about its appearance.'[43] There is no attempt to reconstruct actual historical events and personages, to provide a specific point in time, or to have real life history enter the drama. There is as a result little internal specificity. There are no references to contemporary affairs, other than in subsidiary visual form. A poster advertises *Mazeppa*, a melodrama popular in the early 1860s, while in the marshal's office a poster announces the

The empty public space of Hadleyville

President's quest for additional forces, presumably providing a Civil War annotation. Confounding Foreman's original intention, a major building clearly visible towards the beginning of the film bears the unmistakeable date '1888'. Similarly, the locomotive which brings Frank Miller to Hadleyville bears the 'Sierra Railroad' title on its tender, indicating the company originally incorporated in 1890 to serve a 50-mile line East of Stockton, California.[44]

There is, likewise, only a small degree of 'external' reference. The authorities who have decreed the release of Frank Miller are 'up north', a reference which sets in train a classic tension between north and south in the aftermath of Civil War. Ben Miller, it appears, has been in Abilene; Amy Fowler is returning to her home in St. Louis. But these names occur as singular references, without any firmer set of meanings than to confer a weak sense of diegetic reality, and to open up a passing sense of a world 'out there'. Out there, when it comes to it, there are few concrete destinations. Will and Amy do not know where they are going when they hurriedly set off on their honeymoon; nor is there any clearer sense, as they once more quit the town at the conclusion of the film, as to where they are now heading.

The film's status as a 'suspense' classic, following on from Wise's structurally related *The Set-Up* (1949), depends upon its increasingly desperate anticipation of the events which will unfold when all its various clocks have reached the time stressed by its title, an effect deepened by the film's apparent maintenance of 'real time'. This is, in fact, illusory; *High Noon* is not Hitchcock's *Rope* (1948), for its 85 minutes of screen time cover a longer 'real' period, judging by the internal times provided by its various clocks. On-screen time tends to run ahead more quickly than running time, so that, for example, there is a gap of some sixteen minutes between Mettrick's departure and Kane's first argument with Harvey Pell, covered in just four minutes' running time. Sometimes the internal clocks reverse the passage of time, so that Harvey Pell goes to the saloon after quitting his job at 11.10, whilst Kane has already gone to warn Helen Ramirez at a time shown to be 11.15. Sometimes time stands still: when Kane goes to the saloon to recruit deputies, the two clocks visible, at either end of the bar, show the same time when he enters and when he leaves. In *High Noon* time takes on a highly existential quality in relation to time past and time future.[45]

Past and Present

What provides the pressure of the present and immediate future is the past. The showdown at noon is the consequence of what happened before in Hadleyville five years ago, when Kane brought Miller to justice for a crime which is not clarified for us, but which earned him a life sentence. He has been paroled, and the chaos wrought in Hadleyville owes much to the fact that, in a further twist of time, the news has taken a week to reach the town, little faster than Frank Miller himself. Frank Miller is thus a figure from the past, a past so vivid that the film's only flashback to an earlier time brings together an image of the now empty chair in which he sat to deliver his final words, here repeated on the sound-track over the image: 'I'll be back!' Frank Miller's 'time' is otherwise unclear in *High Noon*. The still more distant past is also the reservoir of other pressures on the present. The gun culture of the past cost the lives of Amy's father and brother, providing the impetus for her Quaker pacifism and for her unwillingness to countenance her new husband's continuing involvement with violence. Her intended departure from Hadleyville for her earlier home in St. Louis is thus itself a return to past times with their own legacy of loss.

Her female counterpoint, Helen Ramirez, has an equally complex and determining relationship to history. Her past is the history of fight for economic independence, as a woman and as a Mexican, in the inhospitable climate of Hadleyville; it is also a sexual and emotional history which has attached her to, and detached her from, the key male figures in the drama: Frank Miller, Will Kane (to whom she has not spoken for a year), and Harvey Pell (whom she rejects in the course of the film). She, too, is threatened by the past, since she is aware that Frank may know of her liaison with his persecutor. The key aspect of these historical relations is that they remain unspecified. We do not know the nature of Frank Miller's crime, the circumstances of Amy's familial loss, or the way in which Will Kane has both entered and departed from Helen's life. The film does not spell these out in what we might call the positivist manner of other films about the later nineteenth century such as Scorsese's *The Age of Innocence* (1993). The world of the protagonists in *The Age of Innocence*, for instance, is emotionally ambiguous and precarious, as in *High Noon*, and yet it is characterised by a high degree of objective detail and subjective texture, because the intention of the film appears to be to describe the tension between individual desire and prevailing social *mores*.

High Noon does not have this socially descriptive purpose where its main characters are concerned; the 'chain of events' is left open and unclear. For one thing, it represents the past in general as a reservoir of danger and complexity, a kind of existential cloud upon the present. Secondly, it is peopled by characters who are potentially volatile and unpredictable. Helen Ramirez, in particular, with her multiple historical allegiances, seems ready for the role of ambiguous *femme fatale*, but the film stops short of permitting her any decisive intervention in its *dénouement*, other than that of providing the sounding-board for Amy in her change of heart. Above all, the secret truths of the past bear down on our hero – who is privy to them all – in a way which in turn shapes his actions. These complexities must be reduced to action, since the film chooses not to explore the psychological dimensions of Will Kane's struggles, other than through the incessantly external attention bestowed upon his suffering face and body, and in the repeated theme-song which renders external an emotional anguish that he cannot speak.

The Short Story

The story upon which *High Noon* was based, John Cunningham's 'The Tin Star', provides the main dramatic framework for *High Noon* although there are some significant alterations of detail, perspective, narrative sequence, and ideological resolution.[46] Key names have changed. Hadleyville is not named, the sheriff is simply 'Doane', and the villainous brothers are the 'Jordans'. These names persisted in the screenplay until and including the final revised version: 'Kane' was introduced when Katy Jurado experienced difficulty pronouncing 'Doane'. The story takes place on a Sunday, but in this case later, starting just before 3.00pm, with tension mounting towards the arrival of the train at 4.10pm. The townsfolk who fill out the film and provide a major discursive texture for its discourses on citizenship are absent from the short story. The central drama is played out entirely between the givers and the breakers of the law – Doane, his deputy Toby, and the Jordan gang.

Subsidiary characterisations have also changed. In Cunningham's story there are no female figures such as Amy and Helen. Instead, the key female character is Cecilia Doane, who died in 1885 at the age of 53. Her absent presence provides the story with its internal diegetic time-world, which the film does not have, and it is Doane's regular Sunday visit to her graveside in the cemetery, in the manner of one of Ford's heroes, that triggers a fateful encounter with the younger Jordan. In the story, there are two deputies. Slater is a coward – but it is Toby who provides the main ideological trajectory for the tale. At the beginning of the story, he is ready to quit, but by the end, he has assumed Doane's mantle and has come to terms with the unrewarding grimness of the lawgiver's role. In certain senses, right down to the final gunfight, Toby is replaced by Amy in the symbolism of 'apprenticeship' which so often marks the western.

The Cunningham story has a certain harshness, but a positive resolution. The confrontation beside Cecilia's grave provides an accidental start to the *dénouement*. Doane's horse runs back into town, where Toby assumes the marshal has been killed; he takes on Jordan, and is already wounded when Doane comes upon the scene. In the film, Amy's crucial intervention is the result of moral choice, and is part of the broader gender and marital discourse of the film. Whereas the film ends with a live marshal throwing down his badge to quit a town with which he can no longer identify, the short story ends with the marshal's death as he protects the injured Toby and takes a bullet aimed to kill the deputy. In spite of Doane's death, the short story ends in a reaffirmation of the values of the system; in spite of Kane's survival, the film ends on a note of pessimism and rejection.

From Script to Screen
If the finished film is very close to Foreman's script, there are still some telling alterations. Contrary to the script, Will Kane does not experiment with suicide by pulling the trigger of an empty gun aimed at his own head, and on the same subject, Helen does not offer Amy a gun with which to defend her husband. This latter exchange, in particular, has been reduced in terms of dialogue. In the script, Helen explains her youthful marriage to Ramirez and the circumstances of her hard-won economic success in Hadleyville, whilst Amy explains her family's negative attitude to her 'feminism' and her healthy disrespect for the legal niceties of the marriage institution. The script does of course contain the eventually abandoned sub-plot, which fills nineteen shots spread out across three segments. In the first (two shots) we are introduced to a second Deputy, Toby, riding through the countryside, intent on reaching Kane's wedding, but willing to untie the prisoner he

is escorting, Ed Peterson, to allow him a smoke. In a second segment, at a waterhole (eleven shots) the prisoner attacks Toby and a fight ensues before he is restrained. The third (eight shots) takes place at what Foreman calls Mendoza's stage station – Ford's *Stagecoach* (1939) was Foreman's stated model for this location. With Peterson tied up, Toby shares a beer with Martinez, who runs the station, and is persuaded to dally a while by a young Mexican woman who offers to wash his shirt. He gives up his plan to arrive in time for the wedding.

Banal in its own terms, the sub-plot would have served a number of dramatic and narrative functions. It would have added to the film's mixture of national and sexual characteristics in creating a contrast to Hadleyville's Helen Ramirez. It would have illustrated the law officer's mundane and also dangerous day-to-day dealings with criminals – 'Look who's here. Wild Bill Hickok' is the young woman's greeting to Toby – which are merely anticipated in the main plot. Toby's journey towards Hadleyville mirrors that of Miller (which, of course, we do not see), but by means of a different mode of transport on which the script makes ironic comment ('Ain't you heard? We got a railroad now' Toby tells Martinez) and which explains the decline of the staging post. Like his fellow Deputy Harvey Pell, Toby is able to take time off from his job to indulge in dalliance – whilst Kane's own romantic relationship is on hold and under pressure. Disconnected from the main body of the film, the sub-plot ends without closure; Toby thinks he has missed the wedding, but we know, which he does not, that a bigger dereliction of duty is at stake.

Music, Melodrama
If the film's preoccupation with the past pushes it towards *film noir*, then its musical dimension is suggestive of melodrama. Here, more than its theme song is at stake. Although 'Do Not Forsake Me ...' had precursors in the use of theme-song ballads – films like Rossen's war film *A Walk In the Sun* (1945) and De Toth's western *Man In the Saddle*, just ahead of *High Noon* at Columbia in 1951 – the song itself plays a complex role, simultaneously supporting and relativising the western values with which the film is concerned. *High Noon*'s musical originality lies, moreover, in its overall departure from Hollywood conventions in three main ways. First, the film does not commence and conclude on a full-orchestral *fortissimo*, but *pianissimo*, with a ballad-singer accompanied only by guitar, accordion and drums. Second, the single theme-tune

becomes part of the dramatic underscore, anticipating Tiomkin's Greek chorus-like ballad for Sturges' *Gunfight at the OK Corral* (1957). The score is virtually monothematic, the tune acting as the source of virtually every bar of the orchestral incidental music. Third, the role of the symphony orchestra changes, with the burden of expression being taken away from the strings. The violins are dispensed with altogether, and the lower strings which remain (violas, celli and double basses) are 'totally subordinate to a wind, brass and piano-dominated sonority. The result is a darker, starker, de-glamourised quality of tone-colour, one that accords perfectly with the nature of the scenario'.[47]

The music-track has other functions too. The wistful song, summarising the main narrative foci of the plot, brings together the themes of marriage and violent masculine confrontation in an especially acute counterpoint. Redolent of potential loss and fear of the future, it cuts across much of the traditional optimism of the genre. It is characterised by a high degree of interiority, a first person address by the hero to his bride appealing for solidarity. Since Amy in fact abandons Kane early in the film, the song thus plays a particularly poignant role in appealing for something not to happen which has, for most of the film, already taken place. The music's expression of inner emotion also performs an important role in relation to Cooper's laconic style: he rarely expresses his emotions, which in a sense find a sung rather than a spoken outlet on the sound-track. The varying ties between the music- and image-track of the film, and the powerful effects of subjectivity, emotionality and gender representation which these entail, suggest that we are, at this level, moving between the worlds of the action-oriented western and the psychologically reflective cinematic melodrama.

4
. . . .
MEANINGS

Intertextual Relations
If Cunningham's short story was its pre-text, then the narrative and symbolic power of the film ensured its entry into wider fields of intertextuality, making its story effectively unending. Shared sources, for example, linked it directly to Mann's *The Tin Star* (1957), also based on

A former lawman (James Stewart) is redeemed when he returns to help the young sheriff (Anthony Perkins) in Mann's alternative version of *The Tin Star*

Genre intertextualities - *High Noon* in outer space:
Sean Connery in *Outland*

Cunningham, whereas some of its intertextual extensions, on the other hand, were predicated on particular forms of reading and response, such as the brusque retort devised by Hawks in *Rio Bravo* (1959).[48] Other instances were based on the film's narrative and generic openness. Its tantalising ending could invite an eventual sequel – Jameson's *High Noon, Part 2: The Return of Will Kane*, starring Lee Majors (1980) – whilst the breadth of its dramatic allegory enabled it to be remade, outside the western, as a science fiction film, and a British one at that – Hyams' *Outland* (1981), starring Sean Connery. In terms of broader media intertextuality, memories and fantasies of *High Noon* went on to influence numerous TV westerns, and comic references would appear in films as various as Brooks' *Blazing Saddles* (1974) and McTiernan's *Die Hard* (1988). Reduced to a resounding and yet now completely abstract reference, it was to bestow its title on episodes of TV drama from *Casualty* to *Hooperman*, whilst, from the fifties onwards, headline writers and cartoonists, from Suez to Solidarity and beyond, continued to make clichéd meaning from the confrontational implications of the film's title.[49]

Analysts and critics are also media makers, and contributors to intertextuality, and in the case of *High Noon* they were not slow to re-place the film in a wide variety of critical contexts. The first known academic contribution came quickly, in the form of an undergraduate essay at Harvard University, considering *High Noon* in the framework of Aristotelian poetics, submitted by a proud father for Zinnemann's consideration.[50] Two decades later, changes in the social climate, and in the cinema's attitudes to sex and violence, prompted Foreman himself to fantasise a scabrous seventies version of *High Noon*, redolent of Peckinpah and Kubrick.[51] Small wonder that the pervasive and even mythic quality of *High Noon* can permit it to be likened, on the one hand, to the hard-boiled fiction of Elmore Leonard, and at the same time, following a different vision, to the religious narrative of Everyman or Christian allegory in general, or that its existential and emotional dimensions – its treatment of such themes as authority and treachery, solitude and incommunicability – should rapidly create their own critical tradition around the film.[52]

Differing the Western
For André Bazin, writing in France in the early 1950s, *High Noon* represented an unusual and not entirely welcome form of postwar

western.[53] In his view the western had reached 'a definitive stage of perfection' as long ago as 1939. It was best exemplified by Ford's *Stagecoach* (1939), a film which struck the ideal balance between 'social myth, historical reconstruction, psychological truth, and the traditional theme of the western *mise-en-scène*'.[54] In and around this year, veteran directors such as Ford, Vidor, Lang, Wyler, and Curtiz contributed to a vibrant genre which was to disappear in wartime, replaced by the 'superwestern' – 'a western that would be ashamed to be just itself, and looks for some additional interest to justify its existence – an aesthetic, sociological, moral, psychological, political, or erotic interest, in short some quality extrinsic to the genre and which is supposed to enrich it'.[55]

Thus Ford's postwar westerns such as *My Darling Clementine* (1946) and *Fort Apache* (1948) represent a 'baroque embellishment of the classicism of *Stagecoach*'; Vidor's *Duel in the Sun* (1946) is marked in terms of content by a new interest in eroticism, and in terms of form by 'spectacular luxury'; *High Noon* fills the form of the western with a content from elsewhere, although Bazin prefers it to Stevens' *Shane* (1953), which foregrounds myth and symbol.[56] Bazin opted for 'frankly commercial' productions, or 'novelistic' films, which retained the traditional themes but enriched them from within 'by the originality of their characters, their psychological flavour, an engaging individuality, which is what we expect from the hero of a novel'.[57] His favourite is Dmytryk's *Broken Lance* (1954), together with King's *The Gunfighter* (1950), Wellman's *Across the Wide Missouri* and *Westward the Women* (both 1951), Ford's *Rio Grande* (1950) and Dwan's *Silver Lode* (1954). 'Lyricism', 'feeling', 'sensibility', and 'sincerity' are Bazin's watchwords, hallmarks of the early western cinema of Triangle which Bazin contrasts with the preciousness and cynicism of the self-conscious superwestern.

For Andrew Sarris, the key American interpreter of the French authorial tradition, the genre was closely associated with heroic individualism, values most closely associated with the work of Ford and Hawks. Sarris perceived the emergence of two other traditions in the genre. The 'liberal antiwestern' commenced with Wellman's *The Ox-Bow Incident* (1943) and embraced such films as *High Noon*, *The Gunfighter*, Wyler's *The Big Country* (1958) and Huston's *The Unforgiven* (1959), which were characterised by 'a denial of the heroic premise of the Western and an application of anachronistic social principles to a milieu traditionally associated with anarchic individualism.' Their tone is 'weary and disgruntled' – here Sarris compares *High Noon* unfavourably with *Rio Bravo* – and they lack personal style.[58] Sarris preferred the second alternative, the 'neurotic' western. Starting with *Duel in the Sun* and Walsh's *Pursued* (1947), this was a cinema of delirium and of libido, often expressed, unlike the more dour antiwestern, through 'bizarre personal styles'. The key films here, for Sarris, were Mann's *The Naked Spur* (1953), Lang's *Rancho Notorious* (1952), Ray's *Johnny Guitar* (1954), Aldrich's *Apache* (1954), Fuller's *Run of the Arrow* (1957), and Penn's *The Left-Handed Gun* (1958).[59]

A more detailed approach to the 'difference' of the post-war western, and to the social standing of the western hero, was eventually provided by Will Wright, who studied the evolving social mythology of the genre by deducing what he regarded as the basic plot structures of the 65 top-grossing westerns between 1931 and 1972. [60] Linking together a Lévi-Straussian approach to social myth with a Proppian notion of narrative morphology, he defines the 'classical', 'vengeance', 'transitional' and 'professional' plots as variations in the ways in which heroes are formulated, their social relations with the society are construed, and the nature of villainy and dealing with villainy are to be understood. His 'classical' plot, which dominated the period 1931-1955, provides a blueprint for the genre as a whole. In this paradigm, the hero enters a social group, but is unknown to the society. He is shown to have an exceptional ability, and the society recognises a difference between themselves and the hero, according him a special status but not yet completely accepting him. A conflict ensues between society and a group of villains, the latter proving stronger. Complicating the triangle, there is often a bond of friendship or respect between hero and villain. When the villains threaten the society, the hero avoids involvement in the conflict but is drawn in when a friend is endangered, leading the hero to fight and defeat the villains. Rendered safe, the society accepts the hero. Wright's key examples are Curtiz' *Dodge City* (1939), Tourneur's *Canyon Passage* (1946), *Duel in the Sun* and Mann's *The Far Country* (1954).

The 'vengeance' plot occurs ten times in Wright's list, largely in the period 1949-1961. Whereas the classical hero joins the society because of his strength and their weakness, the vengeance hero leaves for the same reason; whilst the classical hero enters his fight because of the values of society, the vengeance hero abandons his fight on the same

grounds. The vengeance plot thus marks 'a steady deterioration' in the relationship between hero and society, as Wright shows in his analysis of *Stagecoach*, Mann's *The Man From Laramie* (1955), Brando's *One-Eyed Jacks* (1961) and Hathaway's *Nevada Smith* (1966). In the early 1950s, however, the relation between the hero and society is significantly changed from the estrangement-acceptance pattern found in both the classical plot and the vengeance variation. This 'transitional' structure does not occur again in any of the westerns on the list of top money-makers, but the new relationships introduced in these films do recur and in the sixties, slightly altered, become the central aspect of Wright's fourth and final narrative structure, the professional plot, where the heroes are hired guns, and the plot is largely taken up with the extended struggle between them and the villains.

For Wright, the three transitional films – *High Noon*, *Broken Arrow* and *Johnny Guitar* – thus represent an inversion of the classical plot. The hero begins in a position within the society, and ends up outside it: Will Kane takes back the marshal's star at the beginning of *High Noon*, yet ends by throwing it away. Society proves stronger than both hero and villains, and the hero's supportive relationship to the society is thus

Transitional westerns:
James Stewart enters Indian society in Daves' antiracist marriage drama *Broken Arrow*

altered: in *High Noon*, his presence complicates their ability to come to an accommodation with the outlaws. The society itself, indeed, may have characteristics – here, moral cowardice and self-interest – which identify it with villainy itself and mean that the hero must fight as much against society as against any formal villains. Women, too, have a new role in this changing structure. Whereas once they served to reconcile the hero to the society, in the transitional western they may have to join the hero, as Amy does, in his fight against society and in his separation from it.

Social Allegories

Wright's method looked on the one hand towards the 'internal' evolution of the genre, and on the other, towards the links between the cinema and the society of the period. This second area of 'real world' connections became the focus for critics interested in *High Noon* less as a contribution to the western genre than in its meaning as a film about the post-war years, as a drama about American society in its national and international relationships. Thus for Peter Biskind, *High Noon* is one of a number of films which model a specific vision of contemporary

Transitional westerns:
saloon boss Joan Crawford withstands territorial pressure in Ray's baroque *Johnny Guitar*

political alternatives in relation to ideas about 'consensus' and 'community'.[61] Unlike Lumet's *Twelve Angry Men* (1957) and Ford's *The Man Who Shot Liberty Valance* (1962), *High Noon* denounces notions of consensus, and attacks 'both centrist models of the community: the federally focused, top-down model favoured by the corporate liberals and the more bottom-up, populist model favoured by the conservatives.'[62] *High Noon*'s vision of potential federation is thus negative. The wider world is absent from the film, except by means of the new technology of the railroad which connects Hadleyville, with its own lack of internal federality, to the very society which has commuted Miller's sentence and set him loose to vent his wrath upon the town he once controlled.

High Noon carves a niche between the twin poles of corporate liberalism and conservatism, and further complicates these binary oppositions. Biskind argues that 'The repudiation of Eastern, so-called civilised values associated with corporate liberalism is much stronger in *High Noon* than it is in conservative films, either *Clementine* or *Liberty Valance*. All three films feature schoolteachers from back East. In *Clementine* and *Liberty Valance*, the male pairs – Earp and Holliday,

Doniphon and Stoddard – compete for the schoolteacher's favours and fight to possess the values she represents. In *High Noon*, she turns out to be wrong. Her values give way to Kane's.'[63] Although Biskind's reading makes good overall sense, he is of course wrong in his belief that Amy Fowler is a teacher; a rather different and more militant persona was envisaged for her in the Foreman text, as we have seen. But this does not detract from Biskind's proposition; Amy does indeed embody many of the qualities associated with the teacher icon.

Biskind is similarly mistaken to argue that, 'aside from its disdain for business values, it would be difficult to tell *High Noon* apart from a right-wing film', since the film in fact offers widely differing portrayals of the world of trade.[64] Those associated with the elder statesmen of the town are seen to be laced with self-interest and with moral cowardice, but other, more acceptable representations of commercial life are also offered in the film. The town's most successful and most sympathetic businessperson, in fact, is none other than Helen Ramirez, whose partner, Mr. Weaver, expresses gratitude for the way in which she has conducted her dealings with him and is delighted to buy her out at a favourable price. It is also the world of small business – in the form of running a store – which Amy has in mind for Kane, a vision of security endorsed at once by the former marshall Martin Howe.

Biskind's claim that *High Noon* is virtually indistinguishable from Siegel's *Dirty Harry* (1971) is thus provocative but too dramatic.[65] It overlooks the widely differing political articulations of the two films, even if the later film also ends with a lawman throwing down his badge in resignation and contempt; Biskind might more usefully have invoked that closer parable of the isolated and alienated lawman, Lang's contemporary thriller *The Big Heat* (1953). He is right, however, to claim that left- and right-wing films of the period often bore a strange resemblance to each other. Radical films, he argues, 'generally obscured the difference between right and left in order to create a broad-based coalition against the centre. They portrayed themselves as above politics, neither right nor left, but just 'moral', and they did so for commercial as well as ideological reasons. The fear of ideological clarity was especially true of left-wing films. By the fifties, they had no real constituency.'[66]

Other commentators have attempted to derive another kind of political significance from *High Noon*. Harry Schein, a contemporary of Bazin, was interested in the post-war evolution of what he saw as the three basic elements – symbolic, psychological, and moral – of the western genre.[67] These elements had intensified, with an excessive interest in the phallic symbolism associated with violent eroticism, and a new deepening of psychological subjectivity. But the evolution of new kinds of moral conflict were for Schein the most fascinating aspect of the change he was observing. Violence, in the new films, posed a new kind of moral problematic, which could have broader social and political dimensions. The 'urgent political message' of *High Noon* could therefore be a form of allegory, in which the community stood in for the United Nations, timorous in the face of the Soviet Union, China and North Korea, with moral courage the sole preserve of the 'very American' sheriff. In this context, while pacifism is a good thing, it must learn the principles of just war. *High Noon*, with its powerful artistry, is thus also for Schein 'certainly the most honest explanation of American foreign policy'. The western genre's uneasy handling of these issues shows it 'grappling with moral problems and an ethical melancholy which could be called existential if they were not shared by Mr. Dulles'.[68]

In the 1970s, the views of Schein and other fifties commentators on this theme were influential in Philip French's formulation of what he dubbed the 'Kennedy' and 'Goldwater' westerns, summed up for him by the polar differences between *High Noon* and *Rio Bravo*. His loose political allegory drew him close to Schein *et al's* reading of the film as an allegory of US intervention in Korea.[69] Although this reading was to baffle and infuriate the film's director in the 1990s, critics such as Schein and French were in fact responding to the ideological ambiguity and pliability of *High Noon*. It came as no surprise to find that one recent commentator, flying in the face of the film's apparent political pedigree, should choose to read the film as endorsing 'the rightness – personified by the use of the right-wing Cooper – of standing up to communism'.[70] But however fertile, these readings were too vague, struggling as they did to anchor a highly abstract film in the complex, shifting patternings of post-war politics. They had no means, other than assertion and allusion, of offering a real context for the film in the detailed politics of Truman's New Deal, and of America's relationship to global politics in the era of the Soviet nuclear threat, the Chinese Revolution and the Korean War.

A different take on social meaning was to anchor the debate more firmly in the immediate question of gender representation in *High Noon*. How did its men and women behave and interact, and what did this tell us about the film's depiction of the social world? The link to a wider politics was clear: for extreme critics of the film, its political meanings, understood as weaknesses, were indeed bound up with its gender vision, specifically its account of masculine behaviour. For Sarris, the film's liberalism was bound up with its lack of verisimilitude in depicting the appliance of the principles of law: Kane would have been more brutal and efficient. For Hawks, the marshal would have been less fearful and would have happily gone ahead under his own steam. For right-wing critics, therefore, the film's politics were conspicuously entwined with its unusual depiction of masculinity.

Sexual Politics

Coming at the issue from the opposite direction, many critics have been tempted, with Molly Haskell, to recall *High Noon* as one of the 'monolithically male' texts of the fifties, a period responsible for fewer films about emancipated women than the preceding decades, and for fewer films about women in general.[71] For Joan Mellen, however, masculinity in the cinema is better understood as coming under new kinds of pressure in this period. The exploration of gender, she suggests, is the outcome of the larger repression of social critique in the context of the Blacklist, as 'Hollywood replaced social dissent with a fascinating and serious examination of *sexual* politics'.[72] For Mellen, in films of the fifties 'we find for the first time since the twenties a host of films offering a complex and nuanced examination of the male psyche. Where men are concerned, the American film turned inward.' In the cinema of the fifties, Mellen argues, images of masculinity were substantially revised: male characters became less action-oriented, more psychologically introspective, even sexually ambivalent.[73]

Symptomatic figures include Kirk Douglas' 'obsessive, misguided hero' in Wyler's *Detective Story* (1951), Bogart's 'grubby, unshaven fifty-year-old' in Huston's *The African Queen* (1951), who 'belches, scratches, smells and blinks with incredulity' on his way to socialisation by Katharine Hepburn, and Delbert Mann's *Marty* (1955), 'one of the only films made in America that took as its central theme and character a man who fulfils *none* of the culture's expectations for the male' (the character in question is played by Ernest Borgnine).[74] In a culture where heterodoxy was discouraged, the cinema acted as an arena where the repressed voice of rebellion could emerge in representations of masculinity which were troubled, alienated, often in revolt, and with a new psychological complexity and sexuality. The key stars of this transformation are Dean and Brando. Brando is the ambiguous Stanley Kowalski of Kazan's *A Streetcar Named Desire* (1951) – part sexual energumen, part child – the impotent paraplegic hero of *The Men*, the innocent rebel bikeboy of *The Wild One*, the self-abjuring revolutionary Emiliano Zapata in Kazan's *Viva Zapata!* (1952), the former prizefighter turned pigeon-fancier Terry Molloy in the same director's *On the Waterfront* (1954). Alongside Brando, Dean offers his own images of the sensitive young man struggling for existential self-definition against the laws of patriarchy (Kazan's *East of Eden*, 1955) and the male peer group (Ray's *Rebel without a Cause*, 1955).

In contrast to these innovatory representations stand films which symbolise an older vision of masculinity. Foremost amongst 'fifties paeans to male strength' is *High Noon*, an 'élitist portrait and demonstration that we should be grateful for stern male leaders wherever we find them'.[75] *High Noon* glorifies the image of the single man of strength and so reverts to 'the most conservative, traditional, and damaging norms of male behaviour as well as to the most romantic myths of

individual effectiveness and group futility'.[76] *High Noon* looks back to
the forties and ahead to the seventies in its vision of personal violence as
a solution to social ills. Collectivity is seen as ineffectual in a film which
includes 'a cynical satire of the democratic process', everyone wanting a
voice but unwilling to take action, in contrast with a hero of few words
but adept at getting things done.[77]

This influential reading does not, however, make much sense of
the wider range of male representations in the film. *High Noon*'s special
slant on men – in which the hero is ageing; cannot make reliable male
alliances; is surrounded by a gallery of men who are either venal, self-
interested, or washed-out; cannot keep his wife; and eventually breaks
down after accepting the inevitability of his own death – fits in poorly
with Mellen's polemical cartoon. A more attuned reading might have
linked the film to those other, troubled images of men that Mellen
correctly perceives to be the major point of evolution in gender
representations in fifties Hollywood. This is the perspective adopted by
Robert Warshow, early in the decade under consideration, in a more
nuanced delineation of the western's representations of masculinity.
Focussing on films stretching from Fleming's seminal *The Virginian*
(1929) to the recent decade and films such as *The Ox-Bow Incident*, *The
Gunfighter*, *High Noon* and *Shane* – and hence linking different stages in
the career of Gary Cooper – Warshow compares and contrasts the figure
of the westerner to that of the gangster, finding them to be the two most
powerful projections of masculinity in contemporary cinema, but with
varied and sometimes opposing moral and ideological values.[78]

The westerner, he suggests, is traditionally a figure of repose, of
leisure, and of unemployment. He is characterised by a sense of
loneliness, and of melancholy. His quest is the defence of a certain kind
of honour, that of 'the last gentleman', and his involvement in violence
occurs in defence of a certain kind of style, of demeanour. In his
relationships with women, he can be shown to be child-like in the face of
Eastern cultural and moral sophistication, but the woman can also be
seen as the child who must learn from him. But the image of the
westerner is also darkened, and made morally ambiguous, by his status
as a killer, so that he sometimes is pushed to the limits of his own moral
framework: 'This mature sense of limitation and unavoidable guilt is
what gives the Westerner a "right" to his melancholy.'[79] By contrast with
the gangster, the Westerner is 'a more classical figure, self-contained and

limited to begin with ... his tragedy lies in the fact that even this circumscribed demand can not be fully realised. ... what we finally respond to is not his victory but his defeat.'[80] As a result, 'the true theme of the Western movie is not the freedom and expansiveness of frontier life, but its limitations, its material bareness, the pressures of obligation'.[81]

This view is very much in tune with the bleak finale of *High Noon*, where Kane's victory over Miller is only partial, since in a deeper sense it also marks his defeat by Hadleyville. It also produces unexpected ideological ramifications. Warshow suggests that the demands of heroism make Kane's isolation tautological, so that the film cannot hold together its interest in heroism on the one hand and its wish to criticise the townsfolk on the other. The result, for Warshow, is a kind of 'vulgar antipopulism'; Kane's fate, he suggests, is not that of tragedy, but merely that of pathos; he is 'the rejected man of virtue'.[82] This may be because, although Warshow does not himself make the connection, Kane is not sufficiently complex a character to bear a 'mature sense of limitation and unavoidable guilt'. In *High Noon*, it is Amy, not Will, whose actual moral principles are compromised and who must cope with her involvement in the act of killing.

Femininities

In *High Noon*, femininity, like masculinity, is also open to critical misunderstanding. The female characters appear, for one thing, to operate according to a conventionalised iconographic contrast. Opposed in national, sexual and emotional styles, Amy's 'Fair Lady' of the North and Helen's 'Dark Lady' of the South create an archetypal contrast which was to recur in yet a further variation when Kelly was paired with Ava Gardner in Ford's *Mogambo* two years later.[83] In the script, however, Amy is no elementary cypher but a complex and autonomous character. She is at odds both with her husband and with her family in St. Louis and by the time she gets aboard the noon train she has lost a father, brother, and a husband. She is heading for an uncertain independence, embodying values very different from the family ethos with which the star was to be associated – this time in contrast with her fellow newcomer Marilyn Monroe – in the trade discourse of the coming period.[84] Her Quakerism itself is a sign of difference, not only from the violence of the law but from the religious orthodoxy of Hadleyville. Indeed, her civil marriage is immediately commented upon when Will goes to the church for help, taken as a sign that the Kanes are outside the norms of mainstream religion and the church.

Amy's evolution takes her through a sudden series of recognitions and misrecognitions which are not explained for us, perhaps signalling once more the film's preoccupation with atmosphere and mood, but its relative lack of interest in psychological analysis. She is drawn from the train by the sound of the gunshot with which Kane has killed Ben, but which Amy involuntarily reads as signalling Will's death. This is the film's only narrative red herring, with the spectator in advance of Amy in knowing that the corpse is not her husband's. Her second moment of change comes when she reads Kane's will, a document withheld from the spectator so that only Kane and Amy are privy to its contents. This is what prompts her third key action, the shooting of Pierce, an action visually withheld from the spectator until the gunman's falling body reveals the killer, Amy, in the background. In her fourth key action, in the final showdown between Kane and Miller, Amy turns from passive hostage to active agent; scratching Miller's face, she struggles from his grasp to allow Kane to carry out the final shooting.

The new bride breaks away as her husband and the judge look on

Amy enters the tense arena of the hotel to await the train

7 8   Amy misrecognises the body: it is not her husband's

The film's concern with gender also intersects with its interests in race and national identity, especially in the figure of Helen Ramirez, the Mexican businesswoman who provides a dramatically different representation of femininity than that of Amy Foster. If the power of the 'Eastern' teacher icon led Biskind into misunderstanding Amy's Quaker pacifism and individualism, then the prevalence of sexualised and eroticised Latin American female types made it easy for critics as astute as Warshow or as authoritative as *The Oxford History of the American West* to fall into a related error by describing Helen as a fallen woman or even, more directly, as a prostitute.[85] She is indeed sexually experienced, linking three of the film's key men (Miller, Kane, Pell), but the film is careful in its delineation of her sexual and economic identities, whilst suggesting that both are rooted in her powerful sense of raced and gendered individuality.

Helen is notable for a number of reasons. There is no sign here of the economic dependence of the stereotype: she is a successful businesswoman who has built up a saloon and a hotel, and who does a rapid business deal with a grateful Mr. Weaver before leaving town. Moreover, it is not clear why and how her relationships with Miller and

Amy confronts the body of the outlaw (Pierce) she has just killed

with Kane have broken down. We know that Miller has been in prison for five years, and that her relationship with Kane, which started later, ended in silence at least a year ago, but Ramirez continues to retain a high degree of emotional independence. Although in the script she is Kane's rejected paramour, it is the simplicity of the final film which, ironically, makes the nature of the personal relations shadowy and ambivalent. It is Helen who becomes the mouthpiece for political judgments about the behaviour of the community in relation both to her own position and to that of Kane.

Whereas a routine perspective on race and representation would simply class her as another instance of the stereotype, a more detailed reading can justifiably regard her portrayal as a 'highly original treatment of a Mexican woman ... No other Mexican woman in modern movies holds the key moral position of Helen Ramirez.'[86] Recent attempts to reclaim *High Noon* for feminism, however, are perhaps too ambitious. Although Joanna Rapf is right to comment that the film's 'subtle subversiveness' puts it ahead of its time, it is not really clear why we should regard the film as being 'strikingly more revolutionary' than contemporary mainstream Hollywood cinema. Rapf's case rests on the proposition that 'women control the point of view of this film', but this is not altogether the case.[87] The major identifications in the film are those of and with Will Kane, introducing in a further modulation, a complex notion of suffering and passive – even 'feminine' – masculinity along the way.

Whilst it is also true that the progressive treatment of women in *High Noon* may be a feature of a broader ideological divergence and variety within the film, as Gwendolyn Foster suggests, it is likewise difficult to agree entirely with her modernist description of the film as 'a metanarrative of difference'.[88] Amy's stance on violence does not really take us any further than Grant's *The Angel and the Badman* (1944), where the Quaker heroine is allowed to make a more fully-fledged case to the recalcitrant John Wayne. Her movement beyond religious dogma is rendered punctually and without dramatic explication – Cooper himself would have an opportunity to explore the dilemma more fully in Wyler's *Friendly Persuasion* in 1958 – and she is once again absorbed into matrimony at the film's conclusion. If the impression left by Helen Ramirez lingers even longer than that of Amy, she, for her part, cannot be reincorporated socially or sexually even when the Miller threat has passed, and she moves out of the film into an uncertain and isolated future because there is no place for her in the stark concluding opposition between the couple and the town.

A different way of understanding gender in *High Noon* is to see the film, with R. Barton Palmer, as an interlocking series of plays on marital consolidation and disruption, in which the heterosexual couple is played off in a dramatic triangle with the social values of the civilised world. In one version of this model, Amy is the disruptive force who unsettles the plot by effectively breaking off her marriage when she rejects her new husband's re-espousal of gun-law. She breaks away – in a gesture of moral defiance striking for the heroine of the period – but is narratively recuperated by the ending of the film, which draws her back into the plot, in an active manner, at the expense of the moral principles which had originally driven her from Hadleyville. This version views the female as in rebellion against the call of a system of law based on violence, then in submission to its needs and herself a participant in its rituals.[89]

We can add to Palmer by suggesting that, in this reading, marriage and domestication are seen as being on the far side of the law, as the destination to which the law-giver aspires when he has reached the limit of his potency as sheriff. A different perspective reverses the polarity. Here, it is Will who is the rebel and who is eventually recuperated. The frame here is the world of marriage and of female domestication. In this context it is Will who breaks the frame when he insists on returning from the countryside to face the Miller gang, but his sojourn in Hadleyville is only temporary. At the end of the film, his journey and his marriage is resumed. Marriage and domestication here are seen not as alternatives to the operations of the law, but in opposition to it. Civilisation is reduced to the culture of the couple, since 'society' turns out to be based not on notions of common interest but of self-interest and fake solidarity.

CONCLUSION

Is there then a single, original and unambiguous *High Noon*? Not really. The film, like any other, existed in a number of states – source, script, object of production, preview text, release text, evaluated object. It passed rapidly into the longer and perennial circuit of re-release, critical and analytic deliberation, and personal and public memory. It then relates in various ways to a number of different worlds: that of its producers' needs and aspirations; that of the depicted world of the American West in the late nineteenth century; that of the fifties world into which it is received; that of the other texts which accompany it, in reality or in the form of more abstract comparisons, in the various contexts in which it is seen and in which reference is made to it, and in the broader and less fathomable subjectivities of its spectators and its critics.

For all the varying and ceaseless social reinscriptions of *High Noon*, its fertility of meaning is, however, not completely open-ended. Going back to some of the conditions of its origins in 1951-3, as I have tried to do, is one possible way of understanding something of the finite nature of this complex and ambiguous cultural product. It is a western, but like so many films within the genre, it is less interested in the historical specifics of the genre than in the contemporary resonances which require a 'double reading' by spectators: it is as much a film about the 1950s as about the closing decades of the nineteenth century. Even then, *High Noon*'s relationship to social issues is by definition oblique and metaphorical. It is indeed a film 'about' the Blacklist, but clearly not in the direct manner of films like Biberman's *Salt of the Earth* (1954) or Taradash's *Storm Center* (1956) with their more direct address to contemporary political realities.[90]

Through the distant prism of the western, *High Noon* meditates on the social realities of its period through somewhat abstract formulations which are difficult to read with any certainty, even when set against the powerful and immediate template of the HUAC drama. Instead, a strong projection of individual moral integrity appears to be favoured in a text powered by the illusion of 'real time' suspense, inflected towards *film noir* (through its preoccupation with the power of the past over the present) and melodrama (through its insistently poignant music-track). That integrity is no longer simply associated with personal power and charisma, rather with suffering and with the loss of personal and social potency, in a substantial revision of masculine identity increasingly typical of the new cinema of the post-war years. Women, for their part, are given stronger and more critical roles which move them beyond commonly perceived sexual and racial steretypes. In the end, matrimony reasserts itself with some difficulty, and in a bleak social vacuum.

We create a different and a lesser film if we reduce the modest intricacies of *High Noon* to assertions about social and political content and position, but we also take the risk of inventing an altogether newer film if we ignore the humble semiotic boundaries of the period by bestowing on the film too much complexity and grandeur. Its dedicated play with the staple semiotics of the genre produces an inventory of characters and their relationships which is, in turn, both routine and innovatory, but is in any case difficult to reduce to a single textual 'subject'. Sometimes ambiguous and even incoherent, it is the sophisticated simplicity of these dealings with the protocols of fifties cinema – from the general institutional pressures of the cinematic institution to the particular demands of narrative and image – which, in my view, guarantee the cultural longevity and mobility of *High Noon*.

Fred Zinnemann

NOTES

....

1 For the director's personal memories, see
Fred Zinnemann, *An Autobiography*, (London:
Bloomsbury Publishing, 1992).
2 Zinnemann, *An Autobiography*, p. 50.
3 Zinnemann, *An Autobiography*, p. 88.
4 Richard Schickel, *Movies* (New York: Basic
Books, 1964), p. 185. For a 50s celebration, see
Richard Griffith, *Fred Zinnemann*, (New York:
Museum of Modern Art, n.d. [1959]). For a
valuable recent anthology of writings about
the director, see the special issue of *Film
Criticism*, vol. 18 no. 3-vol 19 no. 1, Spring-
Fall 1994, and, for a compact pictorial
overview, the special supplement on
Zinnemann published with *Sight and Sound*,
vol. 6 no. 1 (New Series), January 1996.
5 On Kramer's life and career, see Donald
Spoto, *Stanley Kramer: Filmmaker* (New York:
Putnam, 1978).
6 For a contemporary report, see Penelope
Houston, 'Kramer and Company', *Sight and
Sound*, vol. 22 no. 1, July-September 1952,
pp. 20-3; on Kramer's speed, see Thomas F.
Brady, 'Hollywood Survey', *New York Times*,
20 March 1949 and 'Hollywood Report', *New
York Times*, 8 January 1950. For details of
Stillman's profits, see 'No Complaints', *New
York Times*, 23 April 1950.
7 For a memoir, see the unpublished interview
transcripts of 1977, intended as the basis for
an autobiography, which are held in the Carl
Foreman Special Collection, British Film
Institute, London. Hereafter 'Foreman,
transcripts'. The collection also contains a
transcript of Foreman's series of four lectures
on the film, 'Anatomy of a Classic: *High
Noon*', delivered at the American Film
Institute in Spring 1976.
8 On Foreman's allegories, see Maurice
Yacowar, 'Cyrano de HUAC', *Journal of
Popular Film*, vol. 5 no. 1, 1976, pp. 68-75.
On Foreman's development as a writer, see
Foreman, transcripts, vols. 5-6. For the early
context, see Nancy Lynn Schwartz and Sheila
Schwartz, *The Hollywood Writers' Wars* (New
York: Knopf, 1982).
9 For an autobiography, see Tiomkin's *Please
Don't Hate Me* (Garden City, New York:

Doubleday, 1959). For a biography, see
Christopher Palmer, *Dimitri Tiomkin: A
Portrait* (London: T.E. Books, 1984).
10 There are numerous accounts of the life
and times of Gary Cooper. See, for example,
Hector Arce, *Gary Cooper: An Intimate
Biography* (New York: William Morrow and
Co, 1979); Stuart Kaminsky, *Coop: The Life
and Legend of Gary Cooper* (New York: St
Martins Press, 1980); Larry Swindell, *The
Last Hero: A Biography of Gary Cooper* (New
York: Doubleday, 1980). For a film-by-film
guide, see Homer Dickens, *The Complete
Films of Gary Cooper* (New York: Citadel
Press, 1970).
11 The *Motion Picture Herald* polls are
accessibly reproduced in Gene Brown, *Movie
Time: A Chronology of Hollywood and the
Movie Industry From Its Beginnings to the
Present* (New York: Macmillan, 1995).
12 'Top Grossers of 1951', *Variety*, vol. 185
no. 4, 2 January 1952 p. 70; 'Good Quota of
"New Faces" Among Top H'wood Directors,
Scripters', *Variety*, vol. 185 no. 4, pp. 1, 71;
'*Show, Vadis*, Top '52', *Variety* vol. 189 no. 5,
7 January 1953, pp. 4, 61; 'Top Grossers of
1952', *Variety* vol. 189 no. 5, 7 January 1953,
p. 61.
13 For a biography of Kelly, see Robert
Lacey, *Grace* (London: Sidgwick and Jackson,
1994). For the views quoted, see Zinnemann,
An Autobiography, p. 100 and Tiomkin, *Please
Don't Hate Me*, p. 234.
14 The schematic narrative which follows is
developed from the statistical data collated by
Joel W. Finler in *The Hollywood Story* (New
York: Crown, 1988). For other accounts, see
David Bordwell, Janet Staiger and Kristin
Thompson, *The Classical Hollywood Cinema:
Film Style and Production to 1960* (London:
Routledge and Kegan Paul, 1985); Otto
Friedrich, *City of Nets: A Portrait of
Hollywood in the 1940s* (London: Headline
Book Publishing, 1987); Douglas Gomery,
*Shared Pleasures: A History of Movie
Presentation in the United States* (London:
BFI, 1992); John Izod, *Hollywood and the Box
Office, 1895-1986* (London: Macmillan, 1988);

Kristin Thompson and David Bordwell, *Film History: An Introduction* (New York: McGraw-Hill, 1994), part 4, 'The Post-War Cinema, 1946-1960s'; and for detailed contemporary information, see the annual *International Motion Picture Almanac* (New York: Quigley).

15 See Tino Balio's two-part history of the studio, *United Artists: The Company Built By the Stars* (Madison, Wisconsin: University of Wisconsin Press, 1976), and *United Artists: The Company That Changed the Film Industry* (Madison, Wisconsin: University of Wisconsin Press, 1987).

16 This account is indebted to Rudy Behlmer's account of the production of *High Noon* in *America's Favourite Movies: Behind the Scenes* (New York; Frederick Ungar, 1982), ch. 15, pp. 269-288, which I have supplemented from a variety of other sources as indicated.

17 Thomas F. Brady, 'Crusade in Hollywood', *New York Times*, 6 March 1949; A..H Weiler, 'By Way of Report', *New York Times*, 10 April 1949; Kramer, 'Of Filmmaking and Independent Film Producing', *New York Times*, 8 May 1949.

18 On the period of the screenplay, see Foreman, 'Anatomy of a Classic', vols 1-2, and Zinnemann, *An Autobiography*, p. 111. On Ben Maddow's involvement, see Pat McGilligan, ed., *Backstory 2: Interview with Screenwriters of the 1940s and 1950s* (Berkeley: University of California Press, 1991), p. 178.

19 Fred Zinnemann, 'Choreography of a Gunfight', *Sight and Sound*, vol. 22 no. 1, July-Sept 1952, pp. 16-17.

20 Zinnemann, *An Autobiography*, p. 109.

21 Zinnemann, *An Autobiography*, p. 101.

22 For the *High Noon* budget-sheets see the *Sight and Sound* supplement on Zinnemann, vol. 6 no. 1 (New Series), January 1996, pp. 14-15.

23 Foreman, transcripts, vol. 1, p. 7.

24 For an account of Foreman's legal preparations, see the account by his lawyer Stanley Cohn which makes up volumes 1-2 of Foreman, transcripts; for the writer's own memories of the period, see vols 8-9. For the

official account of Foreman's hearing, see US Congress, House Committees on Un-American Activities, *Communist Infiltration of the Hollywood Motion-Picture Industry*, *Hearings*, 82nd Congress, 1951, pts V-VI, pp. 1753-1771. Victor S. Navasky gives a report on the complexities of the Foreman case in *Naming Names* (New York: Viking Press, 1980), ch. 6, 'Guilty Bystanders', especially pp. 156-165. Robert Vaughn provides a valuable broad account of this round of hearings in *Only Victims: A Study of Show Business Blacklisting* (New York: G.P. Putnam's Sons, 1972), ch. IV, 'John S. Wood's Marathon Ten-Part 1951-1952 Investigation of Communism in the Entertainment Field', pp. 118-179. For an overall picture, see David Caute, *The Great Fear: The Anti-Communist Purge Under Truman and Eisenhower* (London: Secker and Warburg, 1978).

25 See Cohn in Foreman, transcripts, vols 1-2.

26 On Cooper's support, and Foreman's concern for Cooper's position, see Cohn in Foreman, transcripts, vols 1-2. On the MPAPAI campaign against the film, see Anthony Holden, *The Oscars: The Secret History of Hollywood's Academy Awards* (London: Warner Books, 1994), rev. ed., pp. 185-8.

27 For a discussion of Wayne's Cold War politics, see Randy Roberts and James S. Olson, *John Wayne: American* (New York: The Free Press, 1995), ch. 13, 'A Different War', pp. 327-355. On Hawks, see 'A Discussion with the Audience of the 1970 Chicago Film Festival' in Joseph McBride (ed), *Focus on Howard Hawks* (Englewood Cliffs, NJ: Prentice-Hall, 1972), pp. 15-16; Carl Foreman, 'On the Wayne', *Punch*, 14 August 1974, pp. 240-2.

28 On Losey's involvement, see David Caute, *Joseph Losey: A Revenge on Life* (London: Faber and Faber, 1994), pp. 104-107. For the Kane/Cooper icon, see *Hollywood Reporter*, vol. 116 no. 26, 29 October 1951, p. 11. On the exhibition context, see 'Selling Approaches: *High Noon*', *Motion Picture Herald*, vol. 188 no. 6, 9 August 1952, p. 39 and 'What the Film

Did For Me', *Motion Picture Herald*, vol. 189 no. 5, 1 November 1952, p. 44.

29 For the background accounts, see Zinnemann, *An Autobiography*, pp. 96-110; Spoto, *Stanley Kramer*, ch. 9, pp. 99-108; Foreman, 'Anatomy of a Classic', vols 1-2; Williams reported in Behlmer, *America's Favourite Movies*, pp. 284-7; Tiomkin, *Please Don't Hate Me*, ch. 23, espec 230-6. For an outsider's account which emphasises the role of Williams, see Swindell, *The Last Hero*, ch. 10, 'The Last Hero', pp. 289-305.

30 On the general institutional context for the song, see Susan Sackett, *Hollywood Sings! An Inside Look at Sixty Years of Academy Award-Nominated Songs* (New York: Billboard Books, 1995), and Donald Clarke, *The Rise and Fall of Popular Music* (London: Penguin, 1995), especially ch. 12, 'The Early 1950s: Frustration and Confusion', pp. 283-312. For a detailed appreciation of Ritter, see Texas Jim Cooper, 'Tex Ritter: His Songs and Personality Expressed Our West', *Films in Review*, vol. 21 no. 4, April 1970, pp. 204-216.

31 For selected contemporary reviews of the film, see '*High Noon* Tense Western with Suspense and Action', *Hollywood Reporter*, vol. 119 no. 5, 30 April 1952, p. 4; 'Brog.', '*High Noon*', *Variety*, vol. 186 no. 8, 30 April 1952, p. 6; Fred Hift, '*High Noon*: A Man Alone', *Motion Picture Herald*, vol. 187 no. 5, p. 1349; '*High Noon*', *Films in Review*, vol. 3 no. 5, May 1952, pp. 243-4; Bosley Crowther, '*High Noon*', *New York Times*, 25 July 1952; Bosley Crowther, 'A Western Legend', *New York Times*, 3 August 1952. For a cool British response, see 'G.L.' [Gavin Lambert?], '*High Noon*', *Monthly Film Bulletin*, vol. 19 no. 221, June 1952, pp. 74-5.

32 'National Box Office Survey', *Variety*, vol. 187 no. 8, 30 July 1952, pp. 3, 8; 'Picture Grosses', *Variety*, vol. 187 no. 8, 30 July 1952, pp. 8-9; 'Six Films Opening This Week in New York', *Hollywood Reporter*, vol. 120 no. 12, 22 July 1952, p. 3; 'Short Product in First Run Houses', *Motion Picture Herald*, vol. 188 no. 5, 2 August 1952, p. 49.

33 'Box Office Champions for 1952', *Motion Picture Herald*, vol. 188 no. 11, 13 September 1952, p. 25.

34 '*High Noon* wins Aug B.O. Stakes; *Jacks* 2nd, Rita – *Affair* 3d, *World* 4th', *Variety*, vol. 187 no. 13, 3 September 1952, p. 4.

35 '750G UA Net as Indies Soar', *Variety*, vol. 189 no. 7, 21 January 1953, pp. 7, 24.

36 'Top Grossers of 1952', *Variety*, vol. 189 no. 5, 7 January 1953, pp. 4, 61.

37 W.R. Wilkerson, 'Trade View', *Hollywood Reporter*, vol. 123 no. 27, 16 March 1953, p. 1.

38 Zinnemann, *An Autobiography*, p. 110.

39 Phil Hardy (ed.), *The Encyclopedia of Western Movies* (London: Octopus Books, 1985), Appendices 1, 2, pp. 364, 365.

40 See Geoffrey A. Brown, 'Putting on the Ritz: Masculinity and the Young Gary Cooper', *Screen*, vol. 36 no. 3, Autumn 1995, pp. 193-213. For a discussion of Cooper's face, see Stuart Hampshire, '*High Noon*', *The Observer*, 2 November 1980. For claims concerning post-production, see Swindell, *The Last Hero*, ch. 10, 'The Last Hero', pp. 289-305.

41 A copy of Zinnemann's annotated script and Foreman's copy containing his outline (hereafter, 'Foreman, *High Noon*'), are lodged in the British Film Institute Library, London. The script has been published in George P. Garrett, O.B. Hardison Jr. and Jane R. Gelfman, (eds.), *Film Scripts Two* (New York: Meredith Corporation, 1971) and Melvin Ward, Michael Werner, (eds.), *Three Major Screenplays* (New York: Globe, 1973). A transcription of the film has been published in Richard Maynard, (ed.), *Values in Conflict* (New York: Scholastic Book Services, 1974). An outline has been published in Leonard J. Leff, *Film Plots: Scene-by-Scene Narrative Outlines for Feature Film Study*, vol. 1 (Ann Arbor, Michigan: The Pierian Press, 1971). These references to Foreman, *High Noon*, pp. 3, 97.

42 Foreman, *High Noon*, p. 3.

43 Foreman, *High Noon*, p. 1.

44 Aaron E. Klein, *Encyclopedia of North American Railroads* (London: Bison Books, 1985), p. 181.

45 Richard Combs, 'When the Big Hand Is On Twelve ... Or 7 Ambiguities of Time', *Monthly Film Bulletin*, vol. 53 no. 269, Jun 1986, p. 188.

46 Cunningham's 'The Tin Star' has been republished a number of times, including, within recent memory, in Bill Pronzini, Martin H. Greenburg (eds.), *The Reel West* (Garden City, New York: Doubleday, 1984) and Stuart Y. McDougal (eds.), *Made Into Movies: From Literature to Film* (New York: Holt, Rinehart and Winston, 1985).

47 I am indebted to Christopher Palmer's discussion of the music of *High Noon* in his chapter on Tiomkin in *The Composer in Hollywood* (London: Marion Boyars, 1976), pp. 118-159 and in his biography *Dimitri Tiomkin: A Portrait* (London: T.E. Books), pp. 92-5. See also William Darby, Jack Du Bois, *American Film Music: Major Composers, Techniques, Trends, 1915-1990* (Jefferson, NC: McFarland and Co, 1990), ch. 8, pp. 229-266.

48 On the relationship between the short story, *High Noon* and *The Tin Star* see Douglas J. McReynolds and Barbara J. Lipps, 'Taking Care of Things: Evolution in the Treatment of a Western Theme, 1947-1957', *Literature/Film Quarterly*, vol. 18 no. 3, 1990, pp. 202-208.

49 For illustrations of this aspect of the film's intertextuality, see Zinnemann, *An Autobiography*, p. 110.

50. Francis D. Thompson Jr., 'Aristotle's Poetics and Zinnemann's *High Noon*', unpublished essay, Harvard University, 1953, Fred Zinnemann Special Collection, Item 15.

51 Carl Foreman, '*High Noon* Revisited', *Punch*, 25 April 1972, pp. 448-450.

52 Howard A. Burton, '*High Noon*: Everyman Rides Again', *Quarterly Review of Film, Radio and Television*, vol. 8, Fall 1953, pp. 80-6; Rémy Hebding, 'Derrière le western, la Bible' (interview with Jean Alexandre), *CinémAction*, no. 80, May 1996, pp. 148-51; Daniel Doniol-Valcroze, 'Un homme marche dans la trahison', *Cahiers du Cinéma*, vol. 3 no. 16, October 1952, pp. 58-60; Patrick Allombert, '*Le train sifflera trois fois (High Noon)*', *Image et son*, no. 269,

1973, pp. 145-8; Steven Albert, 'The Shootist: Redemption of Discredited Authority', *Jump Cut*, no. 26, December 1981, pp. 9-12. See also see Martin Linz's monograph, '*High Noon*': *Literaturwissenschaft als Medienwissenschaft* (Tübingen: Max Niemeyer Verlag, 1983), for an industrious reading of *High Noon* within the German context.

53 André Bazin, 'The Evolution of the Western' (1955) in *What Is Cinema?*, vol. 2 (Berkeley: University of California Press, 1971), pp. 149-157.

54 Bazin, 'The Evolution of the Western', p. 149.

55. Bazin, 'The Evolution of the Western', p. 151.

56 Bazin, 'The Evolution of the Western', pp. 150, 151, 152

57 Bazin, 'The Evolution of the Western', pp. 153, 155.

58 Andrew Sarris, 'The World of Howard Hawks' (1962), in Joseph McBride (ed), *Focus on Howard Hawks* (Englewood Cliffs, NJ: Prentice-Hall, 1972), p. 58.

59 Sarris, 'The World of Howard Hawks', p. 59.

60 Will Wright, *Sixguns and Society: A Structural Study of the Western* (Berkeley: University of California Press, 1975). For a critical view of Wright, and an amplification of the 'transitional' theme, see John Lenihan, *Showdown: Confronting Modern America in the Western Film* (Urbana: University of Illinois Press, 1980).

61 Peter Biskind, *Seeing Is Believing: How America Taught Us to Stop Worrying and Love the Fifties* (New York: Pantheon Books, 1983).

62 Biskind, *Seeing Is Believing*, p. 47.

63 Ibid.

64 Biskind, *Seeing Is Believing*, p. 48.

65 Ibid.

66 Ibid.

67 Harry Schein, 'The Olympian Cowboy', *American Scholar*, vol. 24 no. 3, Summer 1955, pp. 309-320.

68 Schein, 'The Olympian Cowboy', p. 316.

69 Philip French, *Westerns* (London: Secker and Warburg, 1977), rev. ed., p. 34.

70 Brian Neve, *Film and Politics in America: A Social Tradition* (London: Routledge, 1992), p. 185.

71 Molly Haskell, *From Reverence to Rape: The Treatment of Women in the Movies* (Chicago: University of Chicago Press, 1987), 2nd ed., p. 271.

72 Joan Mellen, *Big Bad Wolves: Masculinity in the American Film* (London; Elm Tree Books, 1978), ch. 6, 'The Fifties', pp. 192.

73 Joan Mellen, *Big Bad Wolves*, p. 189.

74 Mellen, *Big Bad Wolves*, pp. 193, 196, 217.

75 Mellen, *Big Bad Wolves*, p. 228.

76 Ibid.

77 Mellen, *Big Bad Wolves*, p. 229.

78 Robert Warshow, 'The Westerner' (1954) in Daniel Talbot (ed.), *Film: An Anthology* (Berkeley: University of California Press, 1972), pp. 148-162.

79 Warshow, 'The Westerner', p. 154.

80 Ibid.

81 Warshow, 'The Westerner', p. 155.

82 Warshow, 'The Westerner', p. 158.

83 John O. Thompson, 'Screen Acting and the Commutation Test', in Christine Gledhill, (ed.), *Stardom: The Industry of Desire* (London: Routledge, 1991), ch. 14, section IV, pp. 186-190.

84 Thomas Harris, 'The Building of Popular Images: Grace Kelly and Marilyn Monroe' (1957), in Gledhill, ch. 4, pp. 40-4.

85 Warshow, 'The Westerner', p. 158; Anne M. Butler, 'Selling the Popular Myth', in Clyde A. Milner II, Carol A. O'Connor and Martha A. Sandweiss, (eds.), *The Oxford History of the American West* (Oxford: Oxford University Press, 1994), pp. 793-4.

86 Arthur G. Pettit, *Images of the Mexican American in Fiction and Film* (College Station: Texas, Texas A and M University Press, 1980), p. 205.

87 Joanna E. Rapf, 'Myth, Ideology and Feminism in *High Noon*', *Journal of Popular Culture*, vol. 23 no. 4, Spring 1990, pp. 75-80.

88 Gwendolyn Foster, 'The Women in *High Noon*: A Metanarrative of Difference', *Film Criticism*, vol. 18 no. 3-vol 19 no. 1, Spring-Fall 1994, pp. 72-81.

89 R. Barton Palmer, 'Masculinist Reading of Two Western Films: *High Noon* and *Rio Grande*', *Journal of Popular Film and Television*, vol. 2 no. 4, Winter 1984-5, pp. 156-162.

90 See Nora Sayre, *Running Time: Films of the Cold War* (New York: the Dial Press, 1982), pp. 175-7.

CREDITS

···························

High Noon

USA
1952
US Copyright Date
30 August 1952
US Release
30 July 1952
US Distributor
United Artists Corporation
UK Tradeshow
24 April 1952
UK Release
9 June 1952
UK Distributor
United Artists Corporation
Production Company
Stanley Kramer
Productions, Inc.
[Producer
Stanley Kramer]
[Associate Producer
George Glass]
Production Supervisor
Clem Beauchamp
Unit Manager
Percy Ikerd
Director
Fred Zinnemann
Assistant Director
Emmett Emerson
Script Clerk
Sam Freedle
Screenplay
Carl Foreman
Based on the magazine story
"The Tin Star" by John W.
(sic; i.e. M.) Cunningham
**Director of Photography
(black and white)**
Floyd Crosby
Head Grip
Morris Rosen
Supervising Editor
Harry Gerstad
Editor
Elmo Williams

Production Designer
Rudolph Sternad
Art Director
Ben Hayne
Set Decorator
Murray Waite
Ladies' Wardrobe
Ann Peck
Men's Wardrobe
Joe King
Make-up
Gustaf Norin
Hairstylist
Louise Miehle
Music/Music Director
Dimitri Tiomkin
Song
"High Noon" by Dimitri
Tiomkin (music), Ned
Washington (lyrics),
performed by Tex Ritter
[Music Arrangements
Dominic Frontiere]
Music Editor
George Emick
Sound Engineer
Jean Speak

7,650 feet
85 minutes

Gary Cooper
Will Kane
Thomas Mitchell
Jonas Henderson
Lloyd Bridges
Harvey Pell
Katy Jurado
Helen Ramirez
Grace Kelly
Amy Fowler Kane
Otto Kruger
Judge Percy Mettrick
Lon Chaney Jr.
Martin Howe
Henry Morgan
Sam Fuller

Ian MacDonald
Frank Miller
Eve McVeagh
Mildred Fuller
Morgan Farley
minister
Harry Shannon
Cooper
Lee Van Cleef
Jack Colby
Robert Wilke
James Pierce
Sheb Wooley
Ben Miller

[*uncredited*]
Tom London
Sam
Howland Chamberlin
hotel clerk
Virginia Christine
Mrs. Simpson
John Doucette
Trumbull
Jack Elam
Charlie
James Millican
Herb Baker
Ted Stanhope
station master
Larry Blake
Gillis
William 'Bill' Phillips
barber
Jeanne Blackford
Mrs. Henderson
Cliff Clark
Weaver
Ralph Reed
Johnny
William Newell
Jimmy
Lucien Prival
bartender
Guy L. Beach
Fred

Virginia Farmer
Mrs. Fletcher
Paul Dubov
Scott
Harry Harvey
Coy
Tim Graham
Sawyer

Nolan Leary
Lewis
Tom Greenway
Ezra
Dick Elliott
Kibbee
Ida Moore
woman in church

Credits checked by Markku
Salmi

The print of *High Noon* in
the National Film and
Television Archive was
acquired specially for the
360 Classic Feature Films
project from Republic
Pictures.

SELECT BIBLIOGRAPHY

1 Unpublished Sources

A Primary Documents

Carl Foreman, script of *High Noon*, British Film Institute Library, London.

Fred Zinnemann, script of *High Noon*, British Film Institute Library, London.

B Secondary Documents

Carl Foreman, 'Anatomy of a Classic', transcripts of four lectures at the American Film Institute, Los Angeles, 1976, held in the Carl Foreman Special Collection, British Film Institute Library, London.

Carl Foreman, Interview Transcripts, 1977, Carl Foreman Special Collection, British Film Institute, London.

Francis D. Thompson Jr., 'Aristotle's Poetics and Zinnemann's *High Noon*', unpublished essay, Harvard University, 1953, Fred Zinnemann Special Collection, British Film Institute Library, London.

2 Books

Hector Arce, *Gary Cooper: An Intimate Biography* (New York: William Morrow and Co. 1979).

Tino Balio, *United Artists: The Company Built By the Stars* (Madison, Wisconsin: University of Wisconsin Press, 1976).

Tino Balio, *United Artists: The Company that Changed the Film Industry* (Madison, Wisconsin: University of Wisconsin Press, 1987).

Rudy Behlmer, *America's Favourite Movies: Behind the Scenes* (New York: Frederick Ungar, 1982).

Eric Bentley, *Thirty Years of Treason* (New York: Viking, 1971).

Peter Biskind, *Seeing Is Believing: How America Taught Us to Stop Worrying and Love the Fifties* (New York: Pantheon Books, 1983).

David Bordwell, Kristin Thompson and Janet Staiger, *The Classical Hollywood Cinema: Film Style and Mode of Production to 1960* (London: Routledge and Kegan Paul, 1985).

Gene Brown, *Movie Time: A Chronology of Hollywood and the Movie Industry From Its Beginnings to the Present* (New York: Macmillan, 1995).

Edward Buscombe (ed.), *The BFI Companion to the Western* (London: André Deutsch, 1988).

Ian Cameron and Douglas Pye (eds.), *The Movie Book of the Western* (London: Studio Vista, 1996).

David Caute, *The Great Fear: The Anti-Communist Purge Under Truman and Eisenhower* (New York: Simon and Schuster, 1978).

David Caute, *Joseph Losey: A Revenge on Life* (London: Faber and Faber, 1994).

Larry Ceplair and Steven Englund, *The Inquisition in Hollywood: Politics in the Film Community 1930-1960* (Berkeley: University of California Press, 1979).

Donald Clarke, *The Rise and Fall of Popular Music* (London: Penguin, 1995).

John Cogley, *Report on Blacklisting*, vol. 1, *Movies*, n.p.: The Fund for the Republic, 1956.

William Darby and Jack Du Bois, *American Film Music: Major Composers, Techniques, Trends, 1915-1990* (Jefferson, NC: McFarland and Co, 1990).

Homer Dickens, *The Complete Films of Gary Cooper* (New York: Citadel Press, 1970).

Joel W. Finler, *The Hollywood Story* (New York: Crown, 1988).

Brandon French, *On the Verge of Revolt: Women in American Films of the Fifties* (New York: Federick Ungar, 1978).

Philip French, *Westerns* (London: Secker and Warburg, 1977) rev edn.

Otto Friedrich, *City of Nets: A Portrait of Hollywood in the 1940s* (London: Headline Book Publishing, 1987).

George P. Garrett, O.B. Hardison Jr., Jane R. Gelfman (eds), *Film Scripts Two* (New York: Meredith Corporation, 1971).

Douglas Gomery, *Shared Pleasures: A History of Movie Presentation in the United States* (London: BFI, 1992).

Richard Griffith, *Fred Zinnemann* (New York: Museum of Modern Art, n.d. [1959]).

Phil Hardy (ed.), *The Encyclopedia of Western Movies* (London: Octopus Books, 1985).

Molly Haskell, *From Reverence to Rape: The Treatment of Women in the Movies*

(Chicago: University of Chicago Press, 1987) 2nd edn.

Anthony Holden, *The Oscars: The Secret History of Hollywood's Academy Awards* (London: Warner Books, 1994) rev edn.

John Izod, *Hollywood and the Box Office, 1895-1986* (London: Macmillan, 1988).

Stuart Kaminsky, *Coop: The Life and Legend of Gary Cooper* (New York: St Martins Press, 1980).

Ephraim Katz, *The Macmillan International Film Encyclopedia* (London: Pan Macmillan, 1994) 2nd edn.

Aaron E. Klein, *Encyclopedia of North American Railroads* (London: Bison Books, 1985).

Robert Lacey, *Grace* (London: Sidgwick and Jackson, 1994).

J. Leff, *Film Plots: Scene-by-Scene Narrative Outlines for Feature Film Study*, vol. 1 (Ann Arbor, Michigan: The Pierian Press 1971).

Richard Griffith, *Fred Zinnemann* (New York: Museum of Modern Art, n.d. [1959]).

John Lenihan, *Showdown: Confronting Modern America in the Western Film* (Urbana: University of Illinois Press, 1980).

Martin Linz, '*High Noon': Literatur-wissenschaft als Medienwissenschaft* (Tübingen: Max Niemeyer Verlag, 1983).

Richard Maynard (ed.), *Values in Conflict* (New York: Scholastic Book Services, 1974).

Pat McGilligan (ed.), *Backstory 2: Interviews with Screenwriters of the 1940s and 1950s* (Berkeley: University of California Press, 1991).

Joan Mellen, *Big Bad Wolves: Masculinity in the American Film* (London: Elm Tree Books, 1978).

Victor S. Navasky, *Naming Names* (New York: Viking Press, 1980).

Brian Neve, *Film and Politics in America: A Social Tradition* (London: Routledge, 1992).

Christopher Palmer, *The Composer in Hollywood* (London: Marion Boyars, 1976).

Arthur G. Pettit, *Images of the Mexican American in Fiction and Film* (College Station, Texas: Texas A and M University Press, 1980).

Randy Roberts, James S. Olson, *John Wayne: American* (New York: the Free Press, 1995).

Richard Schickel, *Movies* (New York: Basic Books, 1964).

N. Schwartz, *The Hollywood Writers' Wars* (New York: Knopf, 1981).

Donald Spoto, *Stanley Kramer: Filmmaker* (New York: Putnam, 1978).

Susan Sackett, *Hollywood Sings! An Inside Look at Sixty Years of Academy Award-Nominated Songs* (New York: Billboard Books, 1995).

Nora Sayre, *Running Time: Films of the Cold War* (New York: The Dial Press, 1982).

Nancy Lynn Schwartz and Sheila Schwartz, *The Hollywood Writers' Wars* (New York: Knopf, 1982).

Larry Swindell, *The Last Hero: A Biography of Gary Cooper* (New York: Doubleday, 1970).

Will Wright, *Sixguns and Society: A Structural Study of the Western* (Berkeley: University of California Press, 1975).

Kristin Thompson and David Bordwell, *Film History: An Introduction* (New York: McGraw-Hill, 1994).

Dimitri Tiomkin, *Please Don't Hate Me* (Garden City, NY: Doubleday, 1959).

US Congress, House Committee on Un-American Activities, *Communist Infiltration of the Hollywood Motion-Picture Industry, Hearings*, 82nd Congress, 1951.

Robert Vaughan, *Only Victims: A Study of Showbusiness Blacklisting* (New York: G.P. Putnam's Sons, 1972).

Melvin Ward and Michael Werner (eds), *Three Major Screenplays* (New York: Globe 1973).

Fred Zinnemann, *An Autobiography* (London: Bloomsbury Publishing, 1992).

3 Chapters and Articles

Steven Albert, '*The Shootist*: Redemption of Discredited Authority', *Jump Cut*, no. 26, December 1981, pp. 9-12.

Patrick Allombert, '*Le train sifflera trois fois (High Noon)*', *Image et Son*, no. 269, 1973, pp. 145-8.

André Bazin, 'The Evolution of the Western' in *What Is Cinema?*, vol. 2 (Berkeley: University of California Press, 1971), pp. 149-157.

Geoffrey A. Brown, 'Putting on the Ritz: Masculinity and the Young Gary Cooper', *Screen*, vol. 36 no. 3, Autumn 1995, pp. 193-213.

Howard A. Burton, '*High Noon*: Everyman Rides Again', *Quarterly Review of Film, Radio and Television*, vol. 8, Fall 1953, pp. 80-6.

Anne M. Butler, 'Selling the Popular Myth' in Clyde A. Milner II, Carol A. O'Connor and Martha A. Sandweiss (eds.), *The Oxford History of the American West* (Oxford: Oxford University Press, 1994), pp. 771-801.

Richard Combs, 'When the Big Hand Is on Twelve .. Or 7 Ambiguities of Time', *Monthly Film Bulletin*, vol. 53 no. 269, June 1986, p. 188.

Texas Jim Cooper, 'Tex Ritter: His Songs and Personality Expressed Our West', *Films in Review*, vol. 21 no. 4, April 1970, pp. 204-216.

Daniel Doniol-Valcroze, 'Un home marche dans la trahison', *Cahiers du Cinéma*, vol. 3 no. 16, October 1952, pp. 58-60.

Carl Foreman, '*High Noon* Revisited', *Punch*, 25 April 1972, pp. 448-450.

Carl Foreman, 'On the Wayne', *Punch*, 14 August 1974, pp. 240-2.

Gwendolyn Foster, 'The Women in *High Noon*: A Metanarrative of Difference', *Film Criticism*, vol. 18 no. 3-vol 19 no. 1, Spring-Fall 1994, pp. 72-81.

Louis Giannetti, 'Fred Zinnemann's *High Noon*', *Film Criticism*, vol. 1 no. 3, Winter 1976-7, pp. 2-12.

Thomas Harris, 'The Building of Popular Images: Grace Kelly and Marilyn Monroe', in Christine Gledhill (ed), *Stardom: The Industry of Desire* (London: Routledge, 1991), ch. 4, pp. 40-44.

Remy Hebding, 'Derrière le western, la Bible' (interview with Jean Alexandre), *CinémAction*, no. 80, 1996, pp. 148-51.

Penelope Houston, 'Kramer and Company', *Sight and Sound*, vol. 22 no. 1, July-September 1952, pp. 20-3.

Howard Hawks (1971), 'A Discussion with the Audience of the 1970 Chicago Film Festival' in Joseph McBride (ed), *Focus on Howard Hawks* (Englewood Cliffs, NJ: Prentice-Hall, 1972), pp. 14-26.

Douglas J. McReynolds, Barbara J. Lipps, 'Taking Care of Things: Evolution in the Treatment of a Western Theme, 1947-1957', *Literature/Film Quarterly*, vol. 18 no. 3, 1990, pp. 202-208.

R. Barton Palmer, 'Masculinist Readings of Two Western Films: *High Noon* and *Rio Grande*', *Journal of Popular Film and Television*, vol. 2 no. 4, Winter 1984-5, pp. 156-162.

Joanna E. Rapf, 'Myth, Ideology and Feminism in *High Noon*', *Journal of Popular Culture*, vol. 23 no. 4, Spring 1990, pp. 75-80.

Andrew Sarris, 'The World of Howard Hawks' (1962), in Joseph McBride (ed), *Focus on Howard Hawks* (Englewood Cliffs, NJ: Prentice -Hall, 1972), pp. 35-64.

Harry Schein, 'The Olympian Cowboy', *American Scholar*, vol. 24 no. 3, Summer 1955, pp. 309-320.

John O. Thompson, 'Screen Acting and the Commutation Test', in Christine Gledhill (ed), *Stardom: The Industry of Desire* (London: Routledge, 1991), ch. 14, pp. 183-97.

Robert Warshow, 'The Westerner' (1954) in Daniel Talbot (ed), *Film: An Anthology* (Berkeley: University of California Press, 1972), pp. 148-162.

Maurice Yacowar, 'Cyrano de HUAC', *Journal of Popular Film*, vol. 5 no. 1, 1976, pp. 68-75.

Fred Zinnemann, 'Choreography of a Gunfight', *Sight and Sound*, vol. 22 no. 1, July-September 1952, pp. 16-17.

4 Trade Periodicals

Hollywood Reporter, 1951-3.
Motion Picture Herald, 1951–3.
Variety, 1951–3.

ALSO PUBLISHED

If you would like further information about future BFI Film Classics or about other books on film, media and popular culture from BFI Publishing, please write to:

BFI Film Classics
BFI Publishing
21 Stephen Street
London W1P 2LN

BFI Film Classics '... could scarcely be improved upon ... informative, intelligent, jargon-free companions.'
The Observer

Each book in the BFI Publishing Film Classics series honours a great film from the history of world cinema. With new titles published each year, the series is rapidly building into a collection representing some of the best writing on film. If you would like to receive further information about future Film Classics or about other books on film, media and popular culture from BFI Publishing, please fill in your name and address and return this card to the BFI*.

No stamp is needed if posted in the UK, Channel Islands, or Isle of Man.

NAME

ADDRESS

POSTCODE

*North America: Please return your card to:
Indiana University Press, Attn: LPB, 601 N Morton Street,
Bloomington, IN 47401-3797

BFI Publishing
21 Stephen Street
FREEPOST 7
LONDON
W1E 4AN